"Aner Govrin is one of the most scholarly psychoanalytic thinkers of our time. In this contemporary critique of the cornerstone of clinical technique, he explores and dissects the many varied interpretations of interpretation itself. Whether as conviction or hubris, epistemological certainty or humility, Govrin casts new critical insight on the very nature of psychoanalytic hermeneutics. This should be mandatory reading for anyone in the field."

Prof. Jon Mills, *author of* End of the World: Civilization and Its Fate

"I wish Aner Govrin's little book on interpretation had been available to me when I was a graduate student and a candidate. And now, too, I am glad to have it. Interpretation intrigues us from the very beginning of our work as psychotherapists, and we never outgrow that sense of wonder, because to study interpretation is to study the birth of meaning. Our fascination with the topic is well served by the kind of fair minded, comparative consideration Govrin gives it. He offers an overview of how interpretation has been conceptualized in the various psychoanalytic traditions; and then, in his excellent final chapter and his afterword, he leads the reader into current controversies and new ideas about interpretation. I know I will recommend this small gem to both students and contemporaries, because its straightforward examination of mysteries will relieve them, on one hand, and encourage their appreciation of the marvels of our work, on the other."

Donnel B. Stern, *Ph.D., William Alanson White Institute*

"Aner Govrin's, *Interpretation: A Contemporary Introduction*, offers an important discussion about this central psychoanalytic concept. As psychoanalysis changes, there are many competing definitions about what interpretation is and how it works, and Govrin rightly points out that they are in need of exploration. He takes us through Freud's idea of interpretation, through the Kleinian development of interpretations of the pre-verbal world of the infant, and includes Betty Joseph's subsequent shift of emphasis from interpretations of the content, to the process between analyst and analysand. He explores Winnicott, as well as Bion's many revolutionary theoretical and clinical ideas, and other contemporary work that provides an overview of how ideas about interpretation have changed. While Freuds and Breuer's so-called 'talking cure' was about verbal interpretation, we see here that as psychoanalysis continues to evolve, there are mysteries in silence to which analysts also need to attend, and interpret. This is a well-needed discussion, and the profound questions that Govrin explores are not easily resolved. He wisely states that his book is 'an invitation to join an on-going conversation.' Those who accept that invitation will be rewarded by new questions and new thoughts about this fundamental aspect of analytic work."

Annie Reiner, *Ph.D., Psy.D., LCSW. Member and senior training analyst, Psychoanalytic Center of California (PCC)*

Interpretation

Interpretation: A Contemporary Introduction invites readers into the evolving heart of psychoanalytic practice, where interpretation stands as both central mystery and transformative tool.

Throughout the book, Aner Govrin traces the evolution of interpretation from Freud's archaeological model of uncovering unconscious wishes, through Klein's immediate interpretive acts in early childhood, Bion's emphasis on containment and creative uncertainty, Winnicott's focus on relational presence, and Kohut's revolution of empathic immersion. Contemporary relational and field theories receive in-depth treatment through analyses of landmark papers and clinical moments that illuminate how interpretation heals, transforms, and sometimes provokes crisis. Rich clinical vignettes and philosophical reflections bring theoretical debates to life, making complex ideas both rigorous and accessible. Readers gain a practical understanding of how different interpretive approaches work in real therapeutic encounters while grappling with fundamental questions about meaning, relationship, and therapeutic change. Far more than a simple technique, interpretation emerges as a paradoxical process that shapes psychic reality and bridges the gap between knowing and not-knowing.

Offering a concise yet thorough introduction to interpretation, this book is the perfect guide for practicing clinicians, graduate students, supervisors, and scholars alike interested in psychoanalysis as both clinical practice and intellectual tradition.

Aner Govrin is a psychoanalyst, philosopher, and clinical psychologist based in Tel Aviv, Israel. He is the director of the doctoral track, 'Psychoanalysis and Hermeneutics', at Bar-Ilan University and is a member of the Tel Aviv Institute for Contemporary Psychoanalysis.

Routledge Introductions to Contemporary Psychoanalysis

Series Editor: Aner Govrin
Executive Editor: Yael Peri Herzovich

Interpersonal Psychoanalysis: A Contemporary Introduction
Anna Maria Loiacono

Psychodynamic and Psychoanalytic Supervision: A Contemporary Introduction
Christine Driver

Couple Relations: A Contemporary Introduction
Mary Morgan

The Oedipus Complex: A Contemporary Introduction
Poul Rohleder

Psychoanalytic Film Theory: A Contemporary Introduction
Ben Tyrer

Thomas Ogden: A Contemporary Introduction
Ofrit Shapira-Berman

Online Psychoanalysis: A Contemporary Introduction
Haim Weinberg

Psychosis: A Contemporary Introduction
Franco De Masi

Interpretation: A Contemporary Introduction
Aner Govrin

For more information about this series, please visit: www.routledge.com/Routledge-Introductions-to-Contemporary-Psychoanalysis/book-series/ICP

Interpretation

A Contemporary Introduction

Aner Govrin

LONDON AND NEW YORK

Designed cover image: © Michal Heiman, Asylum 1855–2020, The Sleeper (video, psychoanalytic sofa and Plate 34), exhibition view, Herzliya Museum of Contemporary Art, 2017

First published 2026
by Routledge
4 Park Square, Milton Park, Abingdon, Oxon OX14 4RN

and by Routledge
605 Third Avenue, New York, NY 10158

Routledge is an imprint of the Taylor & Francis Group, an informa business

British Library Cataloguing in Publication Data
A catalogue record for this book is available from the British Library

Library of Congress Cataloging-in-Publication Data
A catalog record has been requested for this book

ISBN: 978-1-032-96805-6 (hbk)
ISBN: 978-1-032-96806-3 (pbk)
ISBN: 978-1-003-59075-0 (ebk)

DOI: 10.4324/9781003590750

Typeset in Times New Roman
by Taylor & Francis Books

To my mother Norit Govrin

Contents

Series Editor's Preface

Routledge Introductions to Contemporary Psychoanalysis is one of the most prominent psychoanalytic publishing ventures of our day. The series' aim is to become an encyclopedia of psychoanalysis, with each entry given its own book. This comprehensive series illuminates the intricate landscape of psychoanalytic theory and practice. In this collection of concise yet illuminating volumes, we delve into the influential figures, groundbreaking concepts, and transformative theories that shape the contemporary psychoanalytic landscape.

At the heart of each volume lies a commitment to clarity, accessibility, and depth. Our expert authors, renowned scholars and practitioners in their respective fields, guide readers through the complexities of psychoanalytic thought with precision and enthusiasm. Whether you are a seasoned psychoanalyst, a student eager to explore the field, or a curious reader seeking insight into the human psyche, our series offers a wealth of knowledge and insight.

Each volume serves as a gateway into a specific aspect of psychoanalytic theory and practice. From the pioneering works of Sigmund Freud to the innovative contributions of modern theorists such as Antonino Ferro and Michal Eigen, our series covers a diverse range of topics, including seminal figures, key concepts, and emerging trends. Whether you are interested in classical psychoanalysis, object relations theory, or the intersection of neuroscience and psychoanalysis, you will find a wealth of resources within our collection.

One of the hallmarks of our series is its interdisciplinary approach. While rooted in psychoanalytic theory, our volumes draw upon insights from psychology, philosophy, sociology, and other disciplines to offer a holistic understanding of the human mind and its complexities. Each volume in the series is crafted with the reader in mind, balancing scholarly rigor with engaging prose. Whether you are embarking on your journey into psychoanalysis or seeking to deepen your understanding of specific topics, our series provides a clear and comprehensive roadmap. Moreover, our series is committed to fostering dialogue and debate within the psychoanalytic community. Each volume invites readers to critically engage with the material, encouraging reflection, discussion, and further exploration. We invite you to join us on this journey of discovery as we explore the ever-evolving landscape of psychoanalysis.

Aner Govrin

Introduction

Interpretation, like the unconscious, the couch, or the Oedipus complex, functions as one of our field's defining brands—a concept so central to psychoanalytic identity that we invoke it worshipfully, as if the mere act of naming it grants therapeutic power. Yet this worship masks a troubling reality: interpretation has become a term so elastic, so overburdened with competing meanings, that it threatens to mean everything and nothing at once.

Walk into any psychoanalytic conference and listen carefully. One analyst speaks of interpretation as the precise articulation of unconscious content. Another describes it as the creation of new meaning through relational encounter. A third insists that interpretation happens not through words but through the quality of presence itself. Each believes in interpretation's transformative power, yet describes fundamentally different phenomena. We have created a Tower of Babel within our own discipline, where the same word carries radically different meanings depending on who speaks it.

To understand what lies beneath these competing definitions, we need to look at what actually happens in the consulting room.

There exists a moment in every analysis when words do something more than convey meaning. Since Freud, it has been defined as having an effect on inner reality by making the unconscious conscious. In so doing, words somehow transform the reality they attempt to describe. A patient speaks of feeling empty, and the analyst responds: "Perhaps the emptiness protects you from knowing how full of rage you are." The emptiness itself changes,

DOI: 10.4324/9781003590750-1

becomes something different, more complex, and alive with possibility—that is exactly what interpretation strives to do. This is the enigma at the heart of psychoanalytic interpretation: it doesn't simply decode what already exists but participates in creating new forms of psychic reality.

What makes interpretation so mysterious is that it operates in the space between knowing and not-knowing, between what can be thought and what resists thinking. Unlike other forms of therapeutic intervention that aim to provide clarity or relief, interpretation often increases complexity, opening questions and sometimes answering them. It works not by eliminating ambiguity but by making ambiguity fertile, transforming confusion from a problem to be solved into a creative space where new meanings can emerge.

From its earliest days, psychoanalysis has recognized that its most powerful tool is also its most paradoxical one. How do we speak about experiences that have never been put into words? How do we interpret what is, by definition, beyond speech? Every attempt to capture unconscious life in language simultaneously reveals and conceals, illuminates and obscures. The very act of interpretation changes what it seeks to understand, rather like a quantum observation that alters the phenomenon being observed.

Consider the bewildering range of effects of what psychoanalysts call interpretation: When Freud told the Rat Man that his obsessional thoughts about rats revealed his unconscious death wishes toward his father, the patient initially recoiled in horror, then gradually came to accept this interpretation as revelatory truth (Freud, 1909, p. 180). When Melanie Klein informed ten-year-old Richard that his drawing of a starfish represented his wish to devour his mother's breast and steal the babies inside her, the boy responded by drawing even more violent pictures, which Klein took as confirmation of her interpretation (Klein, 1961, p. 23). When Winnicott (1986) sat in silence with a regressed patient for entire sessions, offering no interpretations at all, it was because interpretation can sometimes be just a way for the analyst to rush things along. For him, what the patient values is not pinpoint correctness in the interpretation, but the analyst's readiness to resonate with the patient.

And when contemporary relational analyst Jody Davies discovered herself enacting with a patient the role of an excited little girl showing off to an admiring parent, she recognized this mutual enactment as co-creating an interpretation that neither could have articulated by themselves (Davies, 1994, p. 157).

What unites these radically different moments across a century of psychoanalytic practice is not a shared theory or technique, but something more fundamental: the conviction that one person can offer something to another that transforms their understanding of themselves. Whether through intellectual insight, primitive confrontation, silent presence, spontaneous engagement, or mutual discovery, each analyst believed—had to believe—that their participation could make a difference. This faith in the transformative power of human understanding and speech remains the beating heart of psychoanalytic interpretation. What has changed is not the essential hope but our appreciation of how mysteriously this transformation occurs, how far it exceeds our theories, and how much it depends on something beyond that which any of us can fully know or control.

This book is about how different psychoanalytic thinkers have wrestled with the concept of interpretation, each in their own distinctive way. It is a book about interpretation—that strange practice by which analysts believe they can help patients to discover meanings they both do and do not already know. But it is also a book about how the very concept of interpretation has been turned inside out, upside down, and thoroughly reimagined over the past century of psychoanalytic thought.

The Organization of This Book

This proliferation of perspectives might seem like theoretical chaos, but I prefer to think of it as creative ferment. The chapters that follow trace major figures who have shaped our understanding of interpretation, each adding their own distinctive voice to the conversation.

We begin, as we must, with Freud (Chapter 1), who established the terms of the debate that continues to this day. His vision of interpretation as the "royal road" to the unconscious set both the possibilities and the problems that subsequent thinkers would inherit. We explore how Freud understood interpretation as a process of translation—from manifest to latent, from symptom to wish, from present suffering to past trauma, from unconscious to conscious—and why this model functioned less as a final edifice than as a block of clay, inviting successive generations of analysts to sculpt it anew, thereby reflecting the contours of their unique vision.

From Freud we turn to Melanie Klein (Chapter 2), who revolutionized interpretation by applying it to the preverbal world of infant experience. Klein's interpretations of children's play—spoken directly to primitive anxieties and fantasies—scandalized many of her contemporaries. Yet her approach opened up new territories for interpretive work, suggesting that the analyst could address layers of experience that preceded language.

Wilfred Bion (Chapter 3) took Klein's insights and transformed them into something even more radical. For Bion, interpretation was not about revealing preexisting truths but about creating the conditions for new thoughts to emerge. His concept of "O"—the unknowable ultimate reality of emotional experience—challenged analysts to abandon their interpretive certainties in favor of what he called "negative capability." As we explore in detail, Bion's approach turns the analyst from an expert decoder into a participant in a shared journey toward meaning that neither analyst nor patient can predict in advance.

Donald Winnicott (Chapter 4) introduced a distinctly different sensibility, one that prioritized play over work, creativity over insight, and being over knowing. His well-known reluctance to interpret—his preference for waiting until the patient discovered their own meanings—represented a profound respect for the patient's own creative capacities. With Winnicott, interpretation is less about unveiling truths than about creating a space where playing can replace knowing, thereby allowing analytic work to remain alive, unfinished, and generative.

Heinz Kohut (Chapter 5) grappled with a paradox, focusing on the development of his ideas on empathy and interpretation. Kohut's lifelong effort to balance authentic empathic understanding with the demands of scientific objectivity ultimately emphasized his shift from traditional interpretive techniques to a therapeutic approach centered on empathic immersion. The chapter explains the difference between "understanding" and "explaining" phases in interpretation, illustrating how therapeutic change depends on the patient's experience of being deeply understood. Contemporary extensions of Kohut's work are explored, showing empathy as an active process of co-created meaning.

The relational approach (Chapter 6) overturned many of the assumptions that had governed classical interpretation. In this paradigm, interpretation is no longer a unilateral act of insight delivered by the analyst, but a collaborative, co-constructed process shaped by both the patient's and the analyst's subjectivities. Analyst neutrality and objectivity are replaced with an emphasis on mutual influence, enactment, and ongoing negotiation of meaning within the therapeutic relationship. Central clinical concepts—such as dissociations, enactment, and self-disclosure—are reconsidered as essential dimensions of the analytic process rather than obstacles or errors. Ultimately, the approach asserts that psychoanalytic change emerges from dialogue, generative relational experience, and the active participation of both partners in meaning-making.

Chapter 7 steps back to examine five essential writings that have shaped contemporary thinking about interpretation: James Strachey, "The Nature of the Therapeutic Action of Psychoanalysis" (1934); Neville Symington, "The Analyst's Act of Freedom as Agent of Therapeutic Change" (1983); Christopher Bollas, "Catch Them Before They Fall: The Psychoanalysis of Breakdown" (2013); Thomas Ogden, "Ontological Psychoanalysis or 'What Do You Want to Be When You Grow Up?'" (2019); and Donnel Stern, "Interpretation: Voice of the Field" (2023).

These are papers that illuminate unexpected angles and overlooked possibilities in the practice of interpretation. Through a close reading of these texts, we discover themes and variations that might otherwise remain hidden in the vast psychoanalytic literature.

Finally, the afterword reflects on a century of psychoanalytic thinking about interpretation, showing that interpretation is less a technique than an act of faith and openness—it depends on the school of thought that regards it as an encounter that holds both meaning and mystery. In the end, interpretation is not mastery but a gesture of hope, a shared attempt to create something new in the analytic relationship.

This book is for those who find themselves caught between certainty and bewilderment—analysts and therapists who know that interpretation matters but aren't quite sure how or why; students who sense that there is something profound at stake in psychoanalytic interpretation but find the theoretical debates perplexing; scholars who want to understand how a practice that seems so simple—one person speaking to another about meaning—has generated such complex and contradictory theories.

But it is also for anyone curious about the strange human capacity to discover meanings we didn't know we knew, to be surprised by our own thoughts, to find words for experiences that seemed beyond language. In exploring how psychoanalysts have understood interpretation, we are exploring fundamental questions about human understanding itself: How do we know what we know? How do we communicate the incommunicable? How do we change through being understood?

My hope is that this book will serve not as a final word on interpretation but as an invitation to join an ongoing conversation about the questions that animated Freud.

Welcome, then, to the paradox. Let us see what sense we can make of it together.

References

Davies, J. M. (1994). Love in the afternoon: A relational reconsideration of desire and dread in the countertransference. *Psychoanalytic Dialogues*, 4(2), 153–170.

Freud, S. (1909). Notes upon a case of obsessional neurosis. In J. Strachey (Ed. & Trans.), *The standard edition of the complete psychological works of Sigmund Freud* (Vol. 10, pp. 151–318). Hogarth Press.

James, W. (1890). *The principles of psychology* (Vol. 1). Henry Holt and Company.

Klein, M. (1961). *Narrative of a child analysis*. Hogarth Press.

Stern, D. B. (2024). Interpretation: Voice of the field. *Journal of the American Psychoanalytic Association*, 71(6), 1127–1148.
Winnicott, D. W. (1965). *The maturational processes and the facilitating environment*. Hogarth Press.
Winnicott, D. W. (1986). *Holding and interpretation: Fragment of an analysis*. Routledge.

Chapter 1

Interpretation in Sigmund Freud's Writings

In June 1900, Freud confessed to his friend Fliess: "Do you suppose that someday one will read on a marble tablet on my house: 'Here, on July 24, 1895, the secret of the dream revealed itself to Dr. Sigm. Freud.' So far there is little prospect of it" (Masson, 1985, p. 417).

What he didn't mention was that the secret, once revealed, would never stop revealing itself—that interpretation, as the uncovering of the unconscious and its modes of functioning, would turn out to be a kind of endless opening.

Consider what happened when Freud interpreted his patient Dora's second dream (Freud, 1905, pp. 106–107). She dreams of her father's death, of arriving too late to the funeral, of a peculiar detail about going upstairs. Freud, with characteristic confidence, explains that this dream is about leaving Herr K., her would-be seducer. The dream is wish-fulfillment disguised as mourning. But Dora, eighteen years old and fed up with being told what she really wants, walks out of the analysis two weeks later. The interpretation was brilliant, systematic, probably even correct. It was also, in some essential way, a catastrophe. It succeeded as correspondence truth—capturing what was factually accurate—yet failed as pragmatic truth, as something that could actually work in the lived reality of the analysis (Yadlin-Gadot, 2016, 2017).

This is where we might begin thinking about psychoanalytic interpretation with this curious fact—that being right about someone else's unconscious can be a form of being wrong about everything that matters. Freud had given Dora the truth, and she

DOI: 10.4324/9781003590750-2

had preferred her symptoms. Or perhaps—and this is what he couldn't quite bring himself to think—she had preferred her own truth to his.

Freud would spend years puzzling over the Dora case, adding footnotes to his failure, interpreting his interpretations. In later works—especially with the advent of the structural model in *The Ego and the Id*—he returned to Dora's analysis as a touchstone for methodological reflection (Freud, 1923). By then, Freud could reconsider his own technical missteps through an evolved lens: he had underestimated the force of unconscious defenses rooted within the ego itself, and he recognized that Dora's refusal was less a simple rejection of his interpretation than a complex act of psychic preservation. In subsequent footnotes and papers, Freud's self-critique revealed a growing humility regarding the analyst's power—a realization that interpretation, without attunement to transference and ego resistance, might fail not because it is "wrong," but because it collides with the patient's need to maintain psychic equilibrium. Thus, Dora's case became a junction between two Freudian eras: from the confidence of uncovering wish-fulfillment to the skepticism that accompanies listening to the ego's defensive architecture.

To understand how Freud reached this impasse with Dora—and how it would eventually transform his entire approach to interpretation—we need to trace the evolution of his method from its confident beginnings to this moment of crisis. The story begins with Freud's belief that he had discovered something like a universal decoder for the unconscious mind.

The Birth of a Method

When Freud first began developing his interpretive method in the 1890s, he was convinced he had found something like a Rosetta Stone for the unconscious. The secret he believed he had discovered was deceptively simple: dreams are wish-fulfillments, and interpretation is the method by which we reverse the dream-work to uncover the forbidden wish hiding within.

However, Freud didn't just claim to interpret dreams; he developed a radically new theory about how meaning itself operates in the human psyche. According to Freud, the unconscious doesn't speak directly. It can't. Instead, it smuggles its messages past the censor through a series of transformations he called the "dream-work": condensation (multiple ideas compressed into one image), displacement (emotional intensity shifted from important to trivial elements), symbolization (abstract thoughts converted to concrete images), and secondary revision (the dreamer's attempt to make sense of the chaos) (Freud, 1900, pp. 277–309).

Every dream, every symptom, every slip of the tongue is essentially a coded message from a part of yourself you can't directly access. Interpretation is the delicate art of decoding these messages without destroying their meaning in the process. It's like trying to understand a poem by translating it word by word into prose—something essential always gets lost.

This sophisticated theory of mental symbolism didn't emerge overnight. Freud's interpretive technique evolved through several distinct phases, each building on the limitations he discovered in the previous approach. The journey from his early cathartic work with Josef Breuer to the fully developed method of free association shows how interpretation as a therapeutic tool had to be forged through trial and error before its theoretical foundations could be established.

From Catharsis to Free Association: The Emergence of Interpretation

Freud's interpretive technique did not emerge fully formed. Its roots lie in the cathartic method developed with Breuer. Hypnosis facilitated the recovery of traumatic memories and their associated affect ("abreaction"), aiming for symptom relief through remembering. Interpretation, during this phase, was rudimentary: the therapist's role was primarily to facilitate access to buried experiences.

The abandonment of hypnosis marked a pivotal shift (Freud, 1914). Freud recognized that resistance—the force opposing the emergence of unconscious material—was the central obstacle. The technique of free association, requiring the patient to verbalize thoughts without censorship (the "fundamental rule"), replaced hypnotic suggestion. This fundamentally changed the interpretive task. The analyst could no longer simply retrieve memories; they had to decipher the patient's communications, which were now distorted by resistance and defense mechanisms. Interpretation became necessary to make sense of associations, slips, dreams, and symptoms—to render the unconscious conscious. As Freud stated, "The physician has to infer the unconscious from what is conscious, employing the technique of interpretation" (Freud, 1923, p. 238).

Between 1900 and 1915, Freud operated with what he called the "topographical" model of the mind, dividing mental life into three regions: the conscious, the preconscious, and the unconscious. In this model, interpretation was essentially archaeological. The analyst was like an explorer excavating buried cities, carefully brushing away layers of defensive sediment to reveal the pristine artifacts of childhood sexuality beneath (Freud, 1915a, p. 173).

"The interpretation of dreams," Freud famously declared, "is the royal road to a knowledge of the unconscious activities of the mind" (Freud, 1900, p. 608).

But if you've been paying attention, you might have noticed something odd here. How can the unconscious be both the thing that needs interpreting and the thing doing the interpreting? This is the kind of paradox that eventually forced Freud to revolutionize his entire theory.

This paradox manifested dramatically in Freud's clinical work. The archaeological model assumed that patients wanted their buried memories uncovered, that resistance was simply an obstacle to be overcome. But Freud's clinical experience told a different story, one that would force him to reconceptualize both resistance and the entire analytic relationship.

The Problem of Resistance and the Transference Revolution

One of Freud's most unsettling realizations was that people themselves—his analysands, eager in theory for relief—became most ingenious at evading it. In the consulting room, the drama was not simply a battle between hidden truth and the analyst's interpretive skill, but a contest between the patient's wish to know and their equally powerful wish not to know. Resistance, in this sense, was not a separate opponent standing at the gates of the unconscious; it was already inside, at work in every gesture, every silence, every apparently innocuous association (Freud, 1912a).

What emerges in *Inhibitions, Symptoms and Anxiety* (Freud, 1926) is the idea that resistance has an economy, a logic, even a kind of creativity. It is the personality's own method for managing what threatens to overwhelm it. To treat resistance only as interference would be to misunderstand it: it is also a message about what cannot yet be borne in words. Freud's shift was to treat resistance itself as a privileged object of interpretation. Before the forbidden wish or the buried scene could be approached directly, the form and function of the resisting had to be understood.

That understanding redefines interpretation. If early technique chased content—"what is hidden here?"—this later refinement starts with process: how is the patient keeping something hidden, and why in this way, now, with me? In this light, the analysis becomes less an excavation than a reading of styles: the avoidance hidden in the overeager disclosure, the evasion embedded in the smallest factual correction. Freud can describe the work of addressing unconscious resistance as bringing it into awareness, then persuading the ego—through reasoning and appeal to its own advantages—to relinquish its defensive hold. But the appeal is never simply rhetorical; it must reckon with the fact that giving up resistance is also giving up a way of surviving.

But Freud's understanding of resistance would prove incomplete until he made the discovery that transformed everything: transference. He noticed that his patients didn't just talk about their past relationships—they recreated them in the consulting room. They fell in love with him, hated him, feared him, idealized him—all for reasons that had nothing to do with who he actually was and everything to do with their unconscious templates for relationships (Freud, 1915b, p. 165).

What Freud gradually came to understand was that transference itself functions as a particularly sophisticated form of resistance. Rather than remembering their past, patients relive it in the present through their relationship with the analyst. They substitute emotional reenactment for mental recollection, replacing the work of memory with the compulsion to repeat. In this way, transference becomes both the medium through which unconscious material emerges and the very mechanism by which the mind avoids truly knowing what it is expressing. The patient who falls passionately in love with the analyst may be expressing their deepest longings, but they are also deflecting from the painful task of understanding where those longings originated and what they truly mean.

This discovery revealed that resistance was never truly free-floating but found its most vivid expression within the transference relationship itself. The patient's reluctance to know was rarely about abstract content but about what knowing would mean here, with this particular listener, in this fragile alliance. The refusals, hesitations, and sudden turns away gained their fullest meaning only when understood as responses to whom these defenses were being directed, and what imagined history was being replayed in the analytic space.

Resistance, as Freud came to understand it, represents the patient's choreography of avoidance, while transference provides the stage on which this choreography is most arrestingly performed alongside the forces that undermine it. The analyst is never a neutral spectator but an unwitting partner in the dance; the evasions, deflections, and sudden openness all find their most concentrated life in the relationship between patient and analyst. The drama of not knowing—the elaborate methods of keeping certain truths at bay—takes shape around the figure of the analyst, who becomes simultaneously the most trusted and most dangerous person in the patient's world.

This insight transformed the nature of interpretation itself. No longer was it enough to decode dreams and symptoms like archaeological artifacts. The analyst had to become a kind of participant-observer, simultaneously involved in and detached from a live re-enactment of the patient's unconscious dramas. Unconscious conflicts and patterns are inevitably re-enacted within the relationship with the analyst. Interpreting the transference—making the patient aware of how past relationships and feelings are being displaced onto the analyst—became the most powerful and direct interpretive tool. "It is on that field [the transference] that the victory must be won" (Freud, 1916–1917, p. 454).

There is, then, a paradox at the heart of resistance: it both thwarts and reveals the ways in which psychic change will be achieved by spelling out psychic defenses. To interpret resistance is to negotiate with the very thing that, if it succeeds in its task, will prevent the negotiation from taking place. But this negotiation inevitably becomes interpretation of transference, not as a separate act but as the same act viewed from another angle. Analysts of the ego psychological tradition took this as a cornerstone: the work of psychoanalysis is to attend to the forms of mind that arise to protect against true psychic truth—forms that crystallize most clearly in the transference relationship. From this perspective, resistance is not the detour from the "real" work—it *is* the work (Freud, 1926).

And perhaps this is what makes interpretation, at its best, feel less like forcing an entry and more like being invited into a conversation the patient has been having all along, with themselves, about whether they dare to speak—a conversation that can only unfold in the presence of another who has become, through transference, both the safest and the most dangerous witness imaginable.

Yet even this sophisticated understanding of resistance and transference left Freud with a troubling theoretical problem. If significant portions of the ego operated unconsciously—as the study of resistance clearly demonstrated—then his original map of the mind was fundamentally flawed. The discovery that patients resisted through unconscious ego defenses demanded nothing less than a complete reconceptualization of psychic structure.

The Structural Revolution

By the 1920s, Freud had concluded that his original topographical model—dividing the mind into the conscious, the preconscious, and the unconscious—no longer adequately explained his clinical findings. Significant portions of the ego were clearly operating outside conscious awareness, and powerful defensive processes emerged as unmistakably unconscious. The elegant geography of the earlier model no longer matched the intricate reality of psychic life.

This recognition led to the formulation of the structural model (Freud, 1923), in which the psyche comprises three functional agencies—id, ego, and superego—each with its own motives, principles of operation, and dynamic relations. The id sought instinctual gratification, the superego imposed moral prohibitions and punitive demands, and the ego was tasked with mediating between internal pressures and external constraints. This new understanding fundamentally transformed both the target and technique of psychoanalytic interpretation.

Under the topographical model, interpretation functioned much like archaeological excavation, with the analyst tracing associations back to latent wishes and uncovering repressed contents (Freud, 1900, pp. 277–309; Freud, 1915a, p. 173). The primary aim was to bring hidden material into consciousness, with resistance manifesting mainly as censorship or repression. The main dangers were misidentifying the psychological artifact or overwhelming the patient with sudden revelations.

The structural model changes the analytic goal, shifting the interpretive focus from what is repressed to how, and by which psychic agency, repression and other defenses are enacted (Freud, 1923, pp. 12–66). The clinician's task is no longer merely to reveal repressed wishes but to analyze the structural interplay—how the ego mediates between id impulses and superego prohibitions, and what defenses it mobilizes in this complex negotiation. Interpretations now targeted the ego's active defenses—intellectualization, repression, projection, rationalization—requiring analysts to understand not just the content of unconscious wishes but the sophisticated defensive strategies employed to manage them.

This shift brought fundamentally new interpretive challenges and dangers. The risk was not only overwhelming the patient with unconscious content but failing to recognize the adaptive function of defenses: interpretation must support the ego's integrative capacity without precipitating destabilization or collapse. The analyst needed to strengthen the ego's ability to manage conflicts among the three agencies, exposing defenses to awareness while helping to reintegrate split-off impulses into the personality. Technique thus moves from exposing buried content toward facilitating the ego's negotiation of internal conflict, making interpretive timing and attunement to defense all the more crucial.

By the time that Freud's account had been published in 1937, the goal of psychoanalysis had evolved to establishing the best possible psychological conditions for the ego's functioning; in achieving that, analysis had fulfilled its purpose. The structural model thus transformed interpretation from a process of translating unconscious material into consciousness to a nuanced engagement with the dynamic interplay of psychic agencies, where the analyst's skill lay not in archaeological excavation but in supporting the ego's ongoing work of psychological integration.

But if the ego's defenses served adaptive functions, and if interpretation needed to support rather than assault these psychological structures, what happened when analysts encountered patients whose earliest experiences had left no accessible memory traces? Freud's late work on construction represents his most ambitious attempt to address this clinical reality—the recognition that some therapeutic work requires building new psychic structures rather than simply uncovering old ones.

From Interpretation to Construction: Freud's Archaeological Vision

Reading Freud's 1937 paper "Constructions in Analysis" reveals a profound shift in his thinking about psychoanalytic technique—one that moves beyond the familiar territory of interpretation into something more ambitious and architectonic. Where interpretation deals with the accessible derivatives of the unconscious, construction attempts something far more audacious: the reconstruction of an entire forgotten world.

Freud's distinction between these two modes of analytic work is not merely technical but philosophical. Interpretation, he suggests, addresses what emerges in the here and now of the session—the slip, the dream fragment, the moment of resistance. It works with what surfaces, with what the unconscious permits to escape through its various disguises. Construction, by contrast, ventures into territory where no direct derivatives exist, where infantile amnesia has created genuine gaps in the psychic record.

The analyst becomes not merely a decoder of symbols but an archaeologist of the mind, piecing together fragments to reconstruct entire civilizations of experience that have been buried beneath layers of repression. Yet Freud notes a crucial difference: unlike the archaeologist who deals with ruins where essential pieces have been irretrievably lost, the psychoanalyst works with a psyche where everything is somehow preserved, waiting to be reconstructed.

This preservation, however, doesn't mean easy access. The analyst must work like a detective assembling a case from circumstantial evidence—character traits, symptoms, patterns of transference, the very shape of the patient's resistances. From these indirect signs, the analyst constructs a narrative of what must have been, offering it to the patient not as definitive truth but as a working hypothesis about their buried history.

What's particularly fascinating is Freud's handling of the patient's response to constructions. Neither simple agreement nor disagreement can be taken at face value. A "yes" might be hypocritical compliance; a "no" might indicate not error but incompleteness. The truth of a construction reveals itself obliquely—through subsequent associations, through dreams that circle around the constructed scenario, through subtle shifts in the analytic atmosphere.

Freud describes those uncanny moments when a construction triggers what he calls "ultra-clear" memories—not of the constructed event itself, but of peripheral details: the wallpaper in a room, the face of a bystander, the furniture arrangement. These vivid but displaced recollections suggest that the construction has touched something real, even if that reality can only be approached sideways, through its atmospheric residue rather than direct recall.

The paper's most provocative turn comes when Freud connects constructions to delusions and hallucinations. Perhaps, he suggests, delusions contain fragments of historical truth—not personal history but the "archaic heritage" of the species. The delusional person, like the analysand responding to a construction, may be struggling to articulate a truth that has no other means of expression. This isn't to validate the delusion's manifest content but to recognize that even in madness, there may be method—and memory. This again emphasizes that even in constructions, Freud did not give up on historical truth and claimed that if we don't unearth it, it will make its own comeback through repetition-compulsion.

This late work of Freud's suggests a psychoanalysis that has moved beyond the simple process of making the unconscious conscious. Construction acknowledges that some experiences leave no retrievable memory traces yet continue to exert their influence through the very structure of personality, through patterns that repeat without ever having been properly experienced in the first place. The analyst must then become a kind of historical novelist, creating plausible narratives that, while they may never achieve the status of recovered memory, can nonetheless produce therapeutic effects through their explanatory power.

The epistemological modesty of Freud's position here is striking. Constructions aim at historical truth but must settle for narrative truth—for stories that make sense of symptoms and suffering even if they cannot claim to represent exactly what happened. The analyst offers these constructions tentatively, ready to revise them as new material emerges, understanding that the goal is not archaeological accuracy but therapeutic efficacy.

In this vision, psychoanalysis becomes a collaborative act of world-building, where analyst and patient together construct a past that can make sense of the present. The construction doesn't recover the past so much as create a usable version of it—one that allows the patient to understand their suffering as historical rather than simply irrational, as having origins even if those origins can never be fully verified.

This is perhaps why Freud ends with that enigmatic connection to collective delusions—those shared human beliefs that, despite contradicting reality, hold extraordinary power over us. These too, he suggests, may derive their force from fragments of historical truth, from the species' own repressed memories. The implication is that construction, whether individual or collective, serves a fundamental human need: to create narratives that connect us to our origins, even when—especially when—those origins remain forever beyond the reach of direct recollection.

This expanded understanding of analytic work—encompassing interpretation, construction, and ego support—inevitably raised practical questions that had troubled Freud from the beginning. If the analyst's interventions could strengthen or weaken psychic structure, if they could facilitate or foreclose therapeutic possibility, then when and how to speak became matters of paramount importance. The question of timing, always central to Freud's technical thinking, took on new urgency in light of these theoretical developments.

The Question of Timing

In his technical papers, Freud became almost obsessive about timing. The analyst must wait, he insisted, until the patient "has come so near to the repressed material that he has only a few more steps to take under the lead of the interpretation you propose" (Freud, 1913, p. 140). Too early, and the interpretation bounces off the patient's defenses like a tennis ball off a brick wall. Too late, and you've missed the moment when insight might have made a difference.

But how do you know when the timing is right? Freud's answer reveals the artistry hidden within his scientific pretensions: you feel it. You sense when the patient's associations are circling around something important, when their resistance has softened just enough to let a new idea in. It's like knowing when to add salt to a soup—too much technique ruins the intuition.

Premature interpretation could overwhelm the ego or strengthen resistance. Freud advised waiting until the material was close to the surface of consciousness and the patient had developed sufficient rapport (positive transference) to tolerate the insight. "One must wait until [the patient] has himself reached the neighbourhood of what he has repressed … one must allow the patient time … to become conversant with the resistance" (Freud, 1913, pp. 139–140).

Freud warned against "flooding" the patient with interpretations. It was preferable to interpret in small, manageable doses, focusing on surface material and resistance before delving into deep content. "It is ... advisable to begin the interpretation of the resistance at the point where it is most easily and clearly manifested" (Freud, 1923, p. 256).

The Living Legacy

Today, more than a century after Freud's first tentative interpretations, we're still grappling with the implications of his discovery. How do we read the coded messages of the unconscious without imposing our own meanings? How do we maintain the necessary asymmetry of the analytic relationship without falling into authoritarianism? How do we honor both the scientific aspirations and the irreducible artistry of interpretation?

These questions don't have easy answers. But perhaps that's the point. Freud's enduring contribution wasn't to solve the riddle of interpretation once and for all but to show us what kind of riddle it is—not a puzzle with a single solution but a living process that reinvents itself with each new encounter.

In the end, what Freud discovered wasn't a method but an ethic: the commitment to take seriously the strangest productions of the human mind, to listen for meaning in apparent meaninglessness, to persist in understanding even when understanding seems impossible. It's a practice that demands both rigor and imagination, both skepticism and faith. Like the unconscious itself, it's always more complex than we think.

And that eighteen-year-old girl who walked out on Freud? She taught him perhaps the most important lesson of all: that the patient, not the analyst, has the last word. Interpretation, no matter how brilliant, only works when it helps people to find their own truth in their own time. Everything else is just words—clever, perhaps, even correct, but missing the point of what it means to truly understand another human being.

Yet questions of technique inevitably raise questions of ethics. The evolution from interpretation to construction, from archaeological excavation to collaborative meaning-making, reflects a fundamental shift in how psychoanalysis conceives the relationship between analyst and patient. Freud did not go that far, but his shift had profound ethical implications that Freud himself was only beginning to explore.

The ethical dimension of interpretation—briefly glimpsed in Freud's acknowledgment that patients have the "last word"—deserves fuller elaboration. Interpretation is fundamentally an act of power: one person claims to know something about another that they cannot know themselves. This asymmetry could easily become authoritarian, even abusive. The analyst holds the supposed key to the patient's suffering, and the patient, vulnerable in their distress, might accept any explanation that promises relief.

Freud's ethical response to this danger was paradoxical: he insisted on both the analyst's authority and its limits. The analyst must maintain "evenly suspended attention" (Freud, 1912b, p. 111), must resist the patient's demands for premature cure or reassurance, and must persist even when the patient protests. Yet simultaneously, the analyst must remain radically uncertain, ready to revise any interpretation, aware that resistance might signal not defensiveness but the patient's legitimate objection to being misunderstood.

This ethical stance requires what we might call "epistemological humility"—the confidence to offer interpretations combined with the humility to hold them lightly. The analyst must believe enough in their perceptions to speak them, yet doubt enough to remain open to correction. It's an ethics of proximity without possession, intimacy without intrusion.

The ethical imperative extends beyond technique to the very conception of cure. If interpretation aimed simply to make patients conform to social norms or the analyst's theoretical framework, it would be a tool of normalization rather than liberation. Freud's radical gesture was to suggest that symptoms have meaning, that suffering makes sense, that even the most bizarre psychological formations deserve respectful attention. The ethics of interpretation thus becomes an ethics of recognition: acknowledging the validity of psychic pain while working toward its transformation.

The dream of interpretation continues. Each generation of analysts rediscovers Freud's insights and their limitations, adding new layers of understanding to the palimpsest. But the fundamental challenge remains the same: how to read the book of the unconscious without tearing its pages, how to illuminate without burning, how to know without possessing. It's a challenge that requires not just intellectual brilliance but something rarer: the wisdom to know when not to interpret, when to let the mystery be.

References

Bernfeld, S. (1932). Der Begriff der Deutung in der Psychoanalyse. *Zeitschrift für angewandte Psychologie*, 42, 448–497.

Etchegoyen, R. H. (1991). *The fundamentals of psychoanalytic technique.* Karnac Books.

Freud, S. (1900). The interpretation of dreams. In J. Strachey (Ed. & Trans.), *The standard edition of the complete psychological works of Sigmund Freud* (Vols. 4–5). Hogarth Press.

Freud, S. (1905a). On psychotherapy. In J. Strachey (Ed. & Trans.), *The standard edition of the complete psychological works of Sigmund Freud* (Vol. 7, pp. 257–268). Hogarth Press.

Freud, S. (1905b). Fragment of an analysis of a case of hysteria. In J. Strachey (Ed. & Trans.), *The standard edition of the complete psychological works of Sigmund Freud* (Vol. 7, pp. 3–122). Hogarth Press.

Freud, S. (1909a). Analysis of a phobia in a five-year-old boy. In J. Strachey (Ed. & Trans.), *The standard edition of the complete psychological works of Sigmund Freud* (Vol. 10, pp. 5–149). Hogarth Press.

Freud, S. (1909b). Notes upon a case of obsessional neurosis. In J. Strachey (Ed. & Trans.), *The standard edition of the complete psychological works of Sigmund Freud* (Vol. 10, pp. 155–318). Hogarth Press.

Freud, S. (1910). The future prospects of psycho-analytic therapy. In J. Strachey (Ed. & Trans.), *The standard edition of the complete psychological works of Sigmund Freud* (Vol. 11, pp. 139–151). Hogarth Press.

Freud, S. (1912a). The dynamics of transference. In J. Strachey (Ed. & Trans.), *The standard edition of the complete psychological works of Sigmund Freud* (Vol. 12, pp. 99–108). Hogarth Press.

Freud, S. (1912b). Recommendations to physicians practicing psycho-analysis. In J. Strachey (Ed. & Trans.), *The standard edition of the complete psychological works of Sigmund Freud* (Vol. 12, pp. 111–120). Hogarth Press.

Freud, S. (1913). On beginning the treatment (Further recommendations on the technique of psycho-analysis I). In J. Strachey (Ed. & Trans.),

The standard edition of the complete psychological works of Sigmund Freud (Vol. 12, pp. 121–144). Hogarth Press.

Freud, S. (1914). Remembering, repeating and working-through. In J. Strachey (Ed. and Trans.), *The standard edition of the complete psychological works of Sigmund Freud* (Vol. 12, pp. 145–156). Hogarth Press.

Freud, S. (1915a). The unconscious. In J. Strachey (Ed. & Trans.), *The standard edition of the complete psychological works of Sigmund Freud* (Vol. 14, pp. 166–215). Hogarth Press.

Freud, S. (1915b). Observations on transference-love (Further recommendations on the technique of psycho-analysis III). In J. Strachey (Ed. & Trans.), *The standard edition of the complete psychological works of Sigmund Freud* (Vol. 12, pp. 157–171). Hogarth Press.

Freud, S. (1916–1917). Introductory lectures on psycho-analysis. In J. Strachey (Ed. & Trans.), *The standard edition of the complete psychological works of Sigmund Freud* (Vols. 15–16). Hogarth Press.

Freud, S. (1918). From the history of an infantile neurosis. In J. Strachey (Ed. & Trans.), *The standard edition of the complete psychological works of Sigmund Freud* (Vol. 17, pp. 1–122). Hogarth Press.

Freud, S. (1920). Beyond the pleasure principle. In J. Strachey (Ed. & Trans.), *The standard edition of the complete psychological works of Sigmund Freud* (Vol. 18, pp. 1–64). Hogarth Press.

Freud, S. (1923). The ego and the id. In J. Strachey (Ed. & Trans.), *The standard edition of the complete psychological works of Sigmund Freud* (Vol. 19, pp. 12–66). Hogarth Press.

Freud, S. (1924). Neurosis and psychosis. In J. Strachey (Ed. & Trans.), *The standard edition of the complete psychological works of Sigmund Freud* (Vol. 19, pp. 147–154). Hogarth Press.

Freud, S. (1926). Inhibitions, symptoms and anxiety. In J. Strachey (Ed. & Trans.), *The standard edition of the complete psychological works of Sigmund Freud* (Vol. 20, pp. 75–174). Hogarth Press.

Freud, S. (1933). New introductory lectures on psycho-analysis. In J. Strachey (Ed. & Trans.), *The standard edition of the complete psychological works of Sigmund Freud* (Vol. 22, pp. 1–182). Hogarth Press.

Freud, S. (1937a). Analysis terminable and interminable. In J. Strachey (Ed. & Trans.), *The standard edition of the complete psychological works of Sigmund Freud* (Vol. 23, pp. 209–254). Hogarth Press.

Freud, S. (1937b). Constructions in analysis. In J. Strachey (Ed. & Trans.), *The standard edition of the complete psychological works of Sigmund Freud* (Vol. 23, pp. 255–269). Hogarth Press.

Grubrich-Simitis, I. (2000). Metamorphoses of *The interpretation of dreams*: Freud's conflicted relations with his book of the century. *International Journal of Psychoanalysis*, 81 (6), 1155–1183.

James, W. (1907). *Pragmatism: A new name for some old ways of thinking*. Longmans, Green & Co.

Masson, J. M. (Ed.). (1985). *The complete letters of Sigmund Freud to Wilhelm Fliess, 1887–1904*. Harvard University Press.

Yadlin-Gadot, S. (2016). *Truth matters: Theory and practice in psychoanalysis*. Brill.

Yadlin-Gadot, S. (2017). (Ef)facing truth: Between philosophy and psychoanalysis. *Journal of Theoretical and Philosophical Psychology*, 37(1), 1–20.

Suggested Reading

Spence, D. P. (1982). *Narrative truth and historical truth: Meaning and interpretation in psychoanalysis*. W. W. Norton & Company.

Chapter 2

Interpretation in Melanie Klein's Writing

Introduction: The Revolutionary Vision

A little boy called Dick, four years old, stands uncertainly at the threshold of Melanie Klein's consulting room. At first, he hardly notices her. When his nurse leaves, he shows no feeling—but over the weeks, a remarkable shift begins. One morning, after violently banging on the cupboard with a spoon, Dick notices some pencil shavings scattered on Mrs. Klein's lap. He pauses, his face clouded with brief concern, and says softly, "Poor Mrs. Klein" (Klein, 1930, p. 33). Here, in the space between aggression and solace, Dick's relationship to his analyst starts to take on emotional weight. Suddenly, Mrs. Klein is no longer a piece of furniture in the room; she is someone who can be hurt, someone he must care for—precisely as Klein's theory foresees: not the absence of feeling, but the coiled intimacy of violent impulse and anxious concern, enacted in the living presence of another.

This vignette encapsulates Melanie Klein's revolutionary contribution to psychoanalytic technique: her conviction that the human mind, from its earliest moments, is engaged in complex object relations characterized by intense love, hatred, and reparative impulses. Where Freud had discovered the child's polymorphous perversity and the violence of infantile wishes, Klein went further, seeing the infant's inner world as populated by part-objects endowed with magical powers and terrifying intentions. Both analysts understood that civilization doesn't tame a wild child; rather, the child desperately constructs defenses

DOI: 10.4324/9781003590750-3

and symbols to manage an inner reality that is, from birth, almost unbearably intense and at odds with civilization.

The Theatre of the Body: Klein's Vision of Infancy

Consider what Klein asked us to imagine: a baby, perhaps six months old, at the breast. For most observers, here is a scene of primal contentment—Madonna and child, the original peace. But Klein saw something else entirely. She saw a battlefield, a passionate drama in which the infant, driven by forces beyond comprehension, attacks, devours, scoops out, and possesses the breast that feeds him, then, overwhelmed by guilt and terror at what he's done, attempts to repair, restore, and resurrect what his own greed has destroyed.

According to Klein, the baby has from birth an innate relationship with the mother (although focusing primarily on her breast) which is imbued with the fundamental elements of an object-relation, that is, love, hatred, phantasies, anxieties, and defences (Klein, 1952, p. 53). Notice what Klein is claiming here: not that the baby develops these capacities, but that they're there from the start, as if human nature came fully equipped with its own tragedy and redemption.

This was Klein's scandalous revision of psychoanalysis: she made the baby interesting. Not cute, not innocent, not even primarily needy—but interesting, complex, already engaged in the fundamental human work of trying to hold together a self that threatens to fragment under the pressure of its own intensity. William James might have recognized this infant—didn't he write that "the baby, assailed by eyes, ears, nose, skin, and entrails at once, feels it all as one great blooming, buzzing confusion"? (James, 1890, p. 488). But where James saw confusion, Klein saw organization—a primitive, phantasmatic organization, but organization nonetheless.

The Theoretical Foundation: Klein's Extension of Freud

Klein's relationship to Freudian theory represents both continuity and radical departure. Like Freud, she believed in the primacy of unconscious phantasy and the centrality of interpretation in psychoanalytic treatment. However, Klein fundamentally revised Freud's developmental timeline and theoretical framework in three crucial ways.

First, Klein postulated that complex object relations exist from birth. This contrasts sharply with Freud's view of primary narcissism and the gradual development of object relations. Second, Klein relocated the Oedipus complex to the first year of life, arguing that oedipal phantasies emerge alongside the depressive position around six months of age. This temporal compression meant that what Freud saw as sequential developmental stages, Klein understood as overlapping positions that the psyche moves between throughout life.

Third, and most significantly for technique, Klein believed that the superego forms much earlier than Freud proposed, emerging in primitive form during the first months of life. This early superego is harsh and persecutory, derived from the infant's own projected aggression. This theoretical revision had immediate technical implications: if such complex mental structures exist from infancy, then even very young children could benefit from deep interpretation.

Klein's revolutionary approach to child interpretation sparked intense debate, most notably with Anna Freud. The dispute between these two pioneers was never simply about technique; it reflected fundamentally different visions of what childhood is and what children need from analysts (Aguayo, 2011). Where Klein saw sophisticated unconscious phantasy life demanding immediate interpretation, Anna Freud saw developmental immaturity requiring careful preparation and gradual introduction to self-understanding. Anna Freud argued that children required a preparatory phase before analysis proper could begin—a period of relationship-building during which the analyst would establish trust and help the child to develop interest in understanding themselves. She worried that premature interpretation could overwhelm the child's immature ego and cause unnecessary anxiety. This debate illuminated a fundamental tension that continues to shape child analysis: the balance between recognizing children's psychological sophistication and respecting their developmental vulnerability.

The Evolution of Klein's Interpretive Technique

Klein's approach to interpretation evolved through her clinical work, beginning with her analysis of her own son Fritz (a practice not uncommon among early analysts, though now recognized as ethically problematic). The first true interpretation in Klein's writings appears when Fritz related his dream-fantasy of the big motor and little motor running into the electric car. Klein explained that "the big motor is his papa, the electric car his mamma and the little motor himself, and that he has put himself between papa and mamma because he would so much like to put papa away altogether and to remain alone with his mamma and to do with her what only papa is allowed to do" (Klein, 1975a, Vol. 1, p. 35). Significantly, Klein calls this an "explanation" and places it in brackets, suggesting her initial uncertainty about this new technical approach.

The evolution from this tentative beginning to Klein's mature technique is dramatic. In interpreting Fritz's negative Oedipus complex, she moved from symbolic allusion to direct naming: "But he is afraid (as he imagines his mamma to be too) that if this stick—papa's wiwi—gets into his wiwi he will be hurt and then inside his belly, in his stomach, everything will be destroyed, too" (Klein, 1975a, Vol. 1, p. 41). This represents a substantial change in which Klein dares to name the organs and functions, translating symbols directly rather than alluding to them. This approach defines simultaneously a theory (that the child understands the semantic value of interpretation), a technique (that symbols must be brought back to their origin), and an ethic (the necessity of telling the child the truth without hiding things) (Etchegoyen, 2005).

The Principle of Immediate Interpretation: The Case of Rita

Klein's most controversial technical innovation was her practice of immediate interpretation. As she recalled in 1955,

> At the time I began to work it was an established principle that interpretations should be given very sparingly. With few exceptions, psychoanalysts had not explored the deeper layers

> of the unconscious—in children, such exploration was considered potentially dangerous.
>
> (Klein, 1975a, Vol. 3, p. 122)

Yet Klein recognized interpretation as the essential instrument of psychoanalysis and applied it unhesitatingly whenever she deemed it necessary.

The case of Rita, whom Klein analyzed in her home in 1923, provides a paradigmatic example. Rita, aged two and three-quarters, entered Klein's consulting room showing signs of acute anxiety. When Rita asked to go to the garden, Klein didn't see this as a simple request for fresh air. She recognized the negative transference dominating the picture. Upon seeing Rita more tranquil in the garden, Klein made a historic interpretation: she told Rita that she feared Klein would do something terrible to her while they were alone in the room, just as she feared at night that a bad woman would attack her in her bed. Within minutes of this interpretation, Rita returned confidently to the playroom.

This interpretation stands as a historical milestone for several reasons. Its precise dating provides certainty about Klein's early technique, and it exemplifies the distinctive characteristics of her approach: the direct address to anxiety, the consideration of transference (including its negative manifestations), and the linking of present behavior to symptoms and underlying conflict (Etchegoyen, 2005, p. 415).

The theoretical justification for immediate interpretation rests on Klein's understanding of anxiety as present from the beginning of life. To delay interpretation is to leave the child alone with terrors they cannot manage. Moreover, Klein believed that accurate interpretation creates rather than depends upon the therapeutic relationship. When a child feels understood at the deepest level, trust follows naturally.

Interpretation as Psychic Nourishment

Klein believed that interpretation itself was a kind of feeding. Just as the infant takes in the mother's milk, so the child patient takes in the analyst's words. And just as milk can be experienced as good or bad, nourishing or poisonous, so interpretations can be felt as helpful or persecutory. The analyst's task isn't simply to be correct but to offer interpretations that can be digested, metabolized, made use of.

This digestive metaphor reveals a profound insight into Klein's understanding of interpretation. It's not primarily a cognitive process—it's a form of psychic nutrition. The child doesn't need to understand the interpretation intellectually; they need to be able to take it in and let it work on them from the inside. This is why Klein could interpret to very young children in language that might seem far beyond their years. She wasn't appealing to their rational understanding but to something more primitive and more powerful.

Klein's clinical material vividly illustrates this process. She recounts the analysis of a child, John, who plays at being a lion and devouring the analyst. Klein doesn't simply observe this play; she interprets his fear of being eaten as a projection of his own aggressive wishes, linking it to early fantasies of devouring the mother and, even earlier, the breast (Klein, 2017a, p. 17). The process of interpretation initially heightens John's anxiety—he becomes more agitated, his play more fragmented—but as the work continues, something shifts. Relief is achieved and new, more trusting forms of play emerge. The interpretation has been metabolized.

The Nature and Function of Kleinian Interpretation

Klein's approach to interpretation is characterized by several distinctive features that differentiate it from classical Freudian technique. First, her interpretations are remarkably concrete, using what Aguayo (2011) calls "anatomical interpretative language" (p. 1117) to describe unconscious phantasies. Where Freud might have spoken of "libidinal cathexis" or "displacement," Klein told children about babies being made and destroyed inside mother's body, about penises being bitten off and devoured, about breasts that persecuted and poisoned. This concreteness reflects Klein's theory that the unconscious speaks in bodily metaphors rather than abstract concepts.

Second, Klein insists that interpretation must always be anchored in the "actual situation and the feelings aroused in this situation," that is, in the here-and-now of the analytic encounter (Klein, 2017b, p. 89). The analyst's task is to clarify the present experience, and only then to make links to the past. Interpretation, for Klein, is never mere guesswork or theoretical imposition but must be grounded in the material currently being explored.

Third, Klein's approach to symbolism represents one of the most controversial aspects of her technique. At the Symposium on Child Analysis in 1927, Klein declared that symbolism "is the lever we must make use of in child-analysis" (Klein, 1975a, Vol. 1, p. 147).

Klein is particularly wary of "enthusiastic beginners" (Klein, 2017a, p. 15) who leap to the deepest or earliest levels of unconscious experience without sufficient justification in the patient's material. She illustrates this with a clinical example: a patient disappointed by being assigned a junior analyst is not to be immediately interpreted as suffering from "breast disappointment"; rather, the disappointment should be linked to more proximate experiences of loss and idealization, such as the disappointment in the father or in subsequent love objects.

Projective Identification and the Interplay of Projection and Introjection

One of Klein's most original contributions to interpretive technique was her understanding of projective identification. This term describes the way in which unconscious phantasies can be communicated from one person to another without words and indeed without conscious awareness.

In Klein's consulting room, interpretation became a way of receiving and returning these projections in modified form. When a child made her feel frightened, angry, or confused, Klein didn't simply note these as countertransference feelings to be analyzed later. She used them as immediate data about what the child was experiencing and trying to communicate.

A child might play at being a strict teacher while casting Klein in the role of naughty pupil. Rather than simply playing along,

Klein might interpret: "You want me to know what it feels like to be small and frightened of someone big and powerful." The interpretation returns the projection but transforms it, making it thinkable rather than merely enactable.

This understanding of interpretation as a form of emotional metabolism revolutionized psychoanalytic technique. The analyst wasn't simply a decoder of symbols but a living container for the patient's most primitive anxieties. Interpretation became a way of demonstrating that these anxieties could be survived, thought about, and ultimately transformed. The analyst must be receptive to the patient's projections, must take them in and process them, but must also maintain sufficient ego strength to return them in a form that can be psychically digested.

Transference as the Gateway to the Unconscious

For Klein, the phenomenon of transference is the "Open Sesame" of analytic work (Klein, 2017b, p. 34). The transference situation—whereby the patient's earliest object relations, conflicts, and fantasies are revived and enacted in the relationship with the analyst—makes the deepest layers of the unconscious accessible. Klein's technical approach is thus rooted in the conviction that "the transference situation and the exploration of the unconscious are the two fundamentals which should continuously guide our technique, and that they are actually interconnected" (p. 34).

Klein is keenly aware of the complexity of transference phenomena. The analyst is not simply a stand-in for the patient's real parents, but is experienced as a composite of multiple internal objects, often rapidly shifting from a benevolent figure to a persecutor, from a real person to a phantastic image. The interplay of love and hate, of positive and negative transference, is at the heart of analytic work. Klein's innovation is to insist that these conflicting feelings are dynamically intertwined: "sorrow, guilt and anxiety are part and parcel of the complex relation to objects which we call love" (Klein, 2017a, p. 8).

Melanie Klein took Freud's idea about transference seriously and extended our understanding of the unconscious process of transference. Central to Klein's revolutionary contribution was her concept of the "total situation" in transference. As she formulated it: "in unraveling the details of the transference, it is essential to think in terms of total situations transferred from the past into the present as well as emotions, defenses and object relationships" (Klein, 1952, p. 437). This understanding meant that transference encompassed not merely isolated feelings or memories, but entire constellations of affects, defensive patterns, and established ways of relating to objects—the complete internal world actualized in the analytic encounter.

Yet paradoxically, despite Klein's theoretical articulation of the total situation concept, her clinical practice revealed a more conservative approach. She primarily employed transference interpretations within a traditional Freudian framework and maintained skepticism toward Heimann's counter-transference formulations (Grosskurth, 1986, p. 382)—elements crucial to understanding the total situation. Even in the *Narrative of a Child Analysis* (Klein, 1961), interpretations addressing the total situation are remarkably sparse. As Hanna Segal observes, Klein herself gave limited attention to exploring countertransference, leaving the full clinical application of the total situation concept to be developed by subsequent generations of analysts.

The Question of Countertransference

Klein's attitude toward countertransference reveals another area where she both extends and departs from Freud. While acknowledging that the patient's projections can profoundly affect the analyst, she maintains a cautious stance: "I have never found that the countertransference has helped me to understand my patient better; if I may put it like this; I have found that it has helped me to understand myself better" (Klein, 2017b, p. 103).

This position might seem to contradict Klein's understanding of projective identification. However, Klein's point is subtle: while the analyst must be receptive to the patient's projections, these must be processed and returned in the form of interpretation rather than enactment. The analyst must maintain a capacity to say "no" to projective identifications that threaten to overwhelm analytic work (Klein, 2017b, p. 105). Klein criticized contemporary uses of projective identification that focus on analyzing the analyst's feelings, insisting instead that the analyst's central task is to use countertransference only as a tool for understanding the patient's internal world, not as an object of exploration in its own right.

The Analytic Attitude: Rigor and Receptivity

Klein's technical approach demands a particular analytic attitude characterized by what she calls an "unfailing desire to ascertain the truth" (Klein, 2017b, p. 5). This orientation requires a balance between critical faculties and emotional openness. The analyst's feelings must be "fully active, though they are kept well under control" (p. 30). Only an analyst who approaches the patient with "deep and true respect for the workings of the human mind and the human personality in general" can hope to facilitate genuine analytic work (p. 30).

Klein warns against feelings of power and superiority, which may arise from the analyst's privileged position. The proper antidote is a "humble and at the same time confident spirit," grounded in the recognition that understanding another person is an extraordinarily difficult enterprise (Klein, 2017b, p. 31).

In her unpublished lectures on technique, Klein provides a more detailed description of what she calls the "analytic attitude," which offers deeper insight into her clinical approach. She describes this as a paradoxical state of mind:

> Our whole interest is focused on one aim, namely, on the exploration of the mind of this one person who for the time being has become the center of our attention ... This rather curious state of mind, eager and at the same time patient, detached from its subject and at the same time fully absorbed in it, is clearly the result of a balance between different and partly conflicting tendencies and psychological drives.
>
> (Klein Archive, cited in Spillius et al., 2011)

This formulation reveals Klein's sophisticated understanding of the analyst's mental position—simultaneously engaged and observing, passionate yet controlled. It suggests that effective interpretation requires not just theoretical knowledge, but a particular quality of attention that can hold contradictions without prematurely resolving them.

Responding to Criticisms

Klein's interpretive approach faced substantial criticism from her contemporaries, particularly regarding three issues: the imposition of theoretical preconceptions, the potential for suggestion, and the appropriateness of deep interpretation with young children.

To the charge of imposing preconceptions, Klein responded empirically: interpretations prove their validity through their effects. When interpretations are accurate, children's play becomes freer, their anxiety diminishes, and their symptoms improve. Klein maintains that children often present adequate material "surprisingly quickly and in great variety" (Klein, 1975a, Vol. 1, p. 134), and interpretation can be given only on the basis of such adequate material.

Regarding suggestion, Klein argued that her technique actually minimizes suggestive influence by addressing unconscious material directly rather than through educative or reassuring measures. The child's subsequent associations, not conscious agreement, validate or invalidate interpretations. The proof was in the pudding—when interpretations were accurate, the clinical material would shift, new themes would emerge, and the child's capacity for symbolization would expand.

As for the appropriateness of deep interpretation with children, Klein's clinical experience demonstrated that children not only tolerate but often welcome interpretations that address their deepest anxieties. The relief of anxiety, achieved through interpretation, opens up new areas of psychic life for exploration. Klein likens anxiety to "explosive material" (Klein, 2017b, p. 16) that must be handled with care, but also asserts that releasing it in manageable quantities is essential to the analytic process.

Klein's Enduring Legacy

Klein's contribution to psychoanalytic technique extends far beyond her specific innovations. She demonstrated that interpretation could be immediate, concrete, and deeply attuned to primitive anxieties. Her work revealed that even the youngest children could benefit from psychoanalytic understanding, provided the analyst could speak the language of the unconscious fluently.

More fundamentally, Klein showed that interpretation is not merely a technical procedure but a form of emotional communication—a kind of psychic feeding in which the analyst's words must be offered in a form that can be taken in, digested, and metabolized. The analyst must be able to receive and process the patient's most primitive projections, returning them in a form that makes the unbearable bearable, the unthinkable thinkable.

Klein's technical innovations—the play technique, immediate interpretation, attention to primitive anxieties, and the systematic analysis of transference—established new possibilities for psychoanalytic treatment. Her fearless approach to the unconscious and her conviction that truth, however painful, is ultimately healing continue to inspire and challenge psychoanalytic practitioners. In Klein's work, interpretation emerges not as an intellectual exercise but as an act of profound emotional engagement, requiring both technical skill and human courage. The analyst must possess not only knowledge but also the capacity to withstand the patient's projections, to think under emotional pressure, and to speak truthfully to a mind in distress.

Later Technical Developments in the Kleinian School

The Kleinian technique continued to evolve significantly after Klein's death. In the 1960s and 1970s, three important trends emerged that modified classical Kleinian practice (Spillius et al., 2011). First, interpretations of destructiveness became more balanced and less focused exclusively on aggression. Second, and perhaps most significantly, the immediate use of interpretations in concrete "part-object" bodily language—speaking directly of attacking breasts or devouring penises—began to be replaced by descriptions of psychological functions such as seeing, hearing, thinking, and evacuating. This shift from anatomical to functional language made interpretations more accessible while maintaining their depth.

Third, the concept of projective identification began to be used more directly in analyzing the transference, with a growing emphasis on enactment in the analyst-patient relationship. This development was particularly important in Betty Joseph's work, which emphasized how patients put pressure on analysts to join in their defensive patterns (Spillius et al., 2011). These changes reflected a growing sophistication in understanding how interpretations are received and processed, rather than focusing solely on their content.

While Klein's innovations revolutionized psychoanalytic technique, questions remained about how interpretations actually create change. How do patients manage to agree with interpretations while remaining untouched by them? Why do some accurate interpretations fail to produce transformation? It was Betty Joseph, working within the Kleinian tradition, who would address these questions by shifting attention from the content of interpretation to the process of how interpretations are received and used—or neutralized—by patients.

Betty Joseph and the Music of Interpretation

There is something profoundly unsettling about the way Betty Joseph listens to her patients. Where Klein and Segal might hear the echoes of ancient phantasies reverberating through the consulting room, Joseph attends to something far more immediate and perhaps more disturbing: the precise way her patient is trying to seduce her into becoming a particular kind of analyst. This shift in listening represents not merely a technical refinement but a fundamental reimagining of what constitutes the most urgent psychological truth in any given moment.

The Shift from Content to Process

The distinction between Joseph's approach and that of her Kleinian predecessors reveals itself most evidently in how each understands the relationship between past and present, between depth and immediacy. Classical Kleinian technique, as exemplified by Hanna Segal and inherited from Klein herself, operates on the assumption that "the deeper the layers of the unconscious reached, the richer and the more stable the therapeutic result" (Segal, cited in Blass, 2011, p. 1151). This approach treats unconscious phantasy as the most immediate and alive element of the patient's experience, requiring direct interpretation to achieve therapeutic change.

As Aguayo (2011) meticulously documents, Klein's technical legacy was built upon "past-to-present transference interpretations in order to effect psychic change" (p. 1117). Both Klein and Segal worked with the patient's "remembered past" and the "unconscious past" (p. 1118)—linking current session material to early infantile phantasies through part-object interpretations.

Where Klein had emphasized the content of interpretation—what was said—Joseph became fascinated by something more elusive: how interpretations were received, used, or discarded by patients. This shift marked her revolutionary departure from the classical tradition. Joseph noticed something that Klein had perhaps been too busy interpreting to see: patients often seemed to agree with interpretations while simultaneously rendering them useless. Joseph gradually "set aside directly linking the patient's past with the present, compelled now by making direct contact with her patients" (Aguayo, 2011, p. 1117).

The Concept of Vertex

Joseph's theoretical framework draws heavily on Wilfred Bion's concept of "vertex"—the organizational perspective from which each person views their world. As Bion (1970) describes: "the psycho-analyst and the analysand each have a vertex (or vertices) which, if it were known, would indicate the organization each regarded as best" (p. 127). In Joseph's formulation (1992), the analyst holds "a theory or theories of desirable psychic change, of what he hopes he may achieve in his work, which is his vertex," while the patient "consciously wishes to change, but dreads any disturbance to his sense of equilibrium, the way in which he deals with anxieties and defences, the organization which he regards as best—this is his vertex" (p. 237).

The therapeutic task becomes finding ways for these two vertices to come together without the patient losing contact with their own experiencing self. As Joseph (1992) explains: "The patient must be able to remain within his own personality organization, looking at things from his own perspective, and yet able to have some part of the self allied with the analyst and thus to look at and begin to recognize his way of operating" (p. 237).

Clinical Illustration: Mr. A. and the Fatal Conceit

Joseph's clinical work with Mr. A., a rigid obsessional man in his mid-thirties, beautifully illustrates her approach. Mr. A. came to analysis "because of severe anxiety and depression following his rejection by a girl colleague" (Joseph, 1992, p. 239). His social life was minimal, he avoided social contacts, and "had difficulty in being away from home and in travelling for more than short periods in trains or planes" (p. 239).

In one pivotal session several years into treatment, Mr. A. brought a dream:

> Mr A was coming down a spiral staircase, carrying a pile of books. He had to hurry to go to a meeting and so put a book down on each step. Afterwards he went back to collect them, but found that one was missing, and felt sure that it had been taken. It was by H, expensive and important to him.
>
> (Joseph, 1992, p. 239)

Joseph doesn't rush to interpret the symbolic meaning of books or staircases. Instead, she tracks how Mr. A. uses the dream material to maintain his psychological equilibrium. When Joseph interprets that she is "stealing away something very precious from him—his omnipotence, his arrogance—and leaving him full of anxieties," Mr. A. suddenly remembers the title of the missing book: *The Fatal Conceit* (Joseph, 1992, p. 240).

Joseph notices something crucial about Mr. A.'s response pattern. Initially, he seems to understand her interpretations, but then his cooperation "became sterile, with him repeating more or less what I said, 'knowing' exactly what was meant, until all movement was paralysed, and a kind of flattened, empty atmosphere was created" (Joseph, 1992, p. 242).

Most tellingly, when the session threatens to become genuinely alive with meaning, Mr. A. shifts to speaking about organizing a memorial for a dead writer—fleeing into grandiosity rather than experiencing the anxiety of real contact. As Joseph observes: "But then there was flight to mania, a somewhat exaggerated and inappropriate idea of a memorial at his workplace. The analyst's perspective is lost and the patient goes 'high'" (Joseph, 1992, p. 242).

The Music of Process

This attention to the micro-processes of the analytic encounter gives Joseph's work an almost musical quality. She emphasizes the importance of monitoring "not only what is being said—the actual words, stories being told—but also to the atmosphere of the session; the pressures on and expectations and anxieties that are being aroused in the analyst" (Joseph, 1992, p. 238).

Joseph's innovation lies in making this very process the focus of interpretation. As Blass (2011) identifies, Joseph's unique contribution is her attention to "the way in which the patient is inviting the analyst to enact and thus maintain his (the patient's) inner dynamics in their current state of equilibrium" (p. 1150). Rather than interpreting what the patient thinks or feels about their past, she interprets how they are actively organizing the analytic relationship in the present moment.

The Challenge of True Psychic Change

Joseph (1992) makes a crucial distinction between genuine insight and intellectual compliance: "If, however, the patient loses contact with his experiencing self, and projectively identifies with, and takes over, the analyst's understanding … then that very understanding becomes an intellectual thing" (p. 243). This is fundamentally different from true understanding, which occurs when "the patient can both remain in contact with what is going on inside himself, while seeing that experience from the analyst's perspective" (p. 243).

This subtle distinction represents Joseph's most significant contribution to psychoanalytic technique. She demonstrates that true psychic change requires maintaining what she calls "a kind of emotional third ear tuned inwards" (Joseph, 1992, p. 238), attending not just to what patients say but to what they do with what is said to them—to the music of the session rather than its lyrics.

Conclusion: Truth, Kindness, and the Limits of Interpretation

The journey from Klein to Joseph reveals both the power and the perils of psychoanalytic interpretation. Klein revolutionized technique by demonstrating that primitive anxieties could be directly addressed, that children and adults alike could tolerate—and benefit from—interpretations of their deepest fears. Joseph refined this approach by shifting focus from what is interpreted to how interpretations are received and metabolized, recognizing that even accurate insights can serve defensive purposes.

Yet both approaches raise fundamental questions about the relationship between truth and kindness in psychoanalytic work. As Kleinian analyst John Steiner observes, "truth can be cruel in its unrelenting logic and it is easy for those who idealise truth to overlook the human limitations that make us depend on illusion in order to survive" (Steiner, 2020, p. 9). This critique applies particularly to certain Kleinian approaches where the analyst's zeal for uncovering aggressive phantasies and negative transference might overshadow recognition of human frailty—both the patient's and the analyst's own.

The danger lies not merely in truth's potential cruelty but in its incompleteness when pursued too rigidly. When analysts become zealots for a particular version of truth—whether Klein's emphasis on primitive aggression or Joseph's focus on defensive processes—they risk what Steiner identifies as a narrow perspective that fails to recognize its own unconscious phantasies. The analyst convinced of their interpretive accuracy may be denying their own sadism, their own need for omnipotent understanding, their own difficulty tolerating the patient's pace of change.

Steiner (2020) cites E. M. Forster who points out that kindness is not just needed to soften the harshness of truth, but also to make the truth itself more authentic and meaningful (p. 10). Steiner thinks that if we approach truth in a rigid or overly narrow way, we may miss the fact that it can sometimes be rooted in unconscious fantasies or denials. By adopting a broader perspective—one that acknowledges human weakness, including our own—a deeper and fuller truth can emerge. This suggests that we should be careful: sometimes an unbending quest for "truth" can turn the analyst into a kind of zealot, idolizing a particular version of truth while overlooking the complexity of the broader situation.

The enduring value of Klein and Joseph lies not in their solutions but in the tensions they illuminate. Klein shows us that avoiding difficult truths serves no one, yet her work also demonstrates how focus on aggression can eclipse recognition of love and reparation. Joseph reveals how patients neutralize even accurate interpretations, yet her meticulous tracking of process might sometimes miss the simple human need for understanding without analysis.

Perhaps true psychoanalytic wisdom lies in holding these tensions rather than resolving them. It requires what neither Klein nor Joseph fully articulated but what their best clinical work embodied: the capacity to pursue truth while respecting necessary illusions, to interpret deeply while recognizing the limits of interpretation, to maintain analytic perspective while acknowledging our shared humanity. This means accepting that sometimes the kindest interpretation is silence, that the deepest truth might be our inability to fully know another person, and that our most therapeutic moments might occur when we abandon our interpretive certainty for genuine encounter with another human being's irreducible mystery.

The evolution from Klein to Joseph thus returns us to a fundamental paradox: psychoanalysis depends on interpretation yet transcends it. The art lies not in perfecting interpretive technique but in discerning when to speak and when to remain silent, when to pursue truth and when to respect protective illusion, when to maintain analytic stance and when to simply be present with another person's pain. This ongoing negotiation—humble rather than zealous, compassionate rather than merely accurate—remains the true challenge of psychoanalytic work.

References

Aguayo, J. (2009). On understanding projective identification in the treatment of psychotic states of mind: The publishing cohort of H. Rosenfeld, H. Segal and W. Bion (1946–1957). *International Journal of Psycho-Analysis*, 90(6), 1115–1133.

Aguayo, J. (2011). The role of the patient's remembered history and unconscious past in the evolution of Betty Joseph's "here and now" clinical technique (1959–1989). *International Journal of Psycho-Analysis*, 92(5), 1117–1136.

Bion, W. R. (1962). *Learning from experience*. Heinemann.

Bion, W. R. (1970). *Attention and interpretation*. Tavistock Publications.

Blass, R. B. (2011). On the immediacy of unconscious truth: Understanding Betty Joseph's "here and now" through comparison with alternative views of it outside of and within Kleinian thinking. *International Journal of Psycho-Analysis*, 92(6), 1137–1157.

Etchegoyen, R. H. (2005). *The fundamentals of psychoanalytic technique* (rev. ed.). Karnac Books.

Feldman, M. (2004). Supporting psychic change: Betty Joseph. In E. Hargreaves & A. Varchevker (Eds.), *In pursuit of psychic change: The Betty Joseph workshop* (pp. 20–37). Routledge.

Grosskurth, P. (1986). *Melanie Klein: Her world and her work*. Alfred A. Knopf.

James, W. (1890). The principles of psychology (Vol. 1). Henry Holt and Company

Joseph, B. (1975). The patient who is difficult to reach. In M. Feldman & E. B. Spillius (Eds.), *Psychic equilibrium and psychic change: Selected papers of Betty Joseph* (pp. 75–87). Routledge.

Joseph, B. (1985). Transference: The total situation. *International Journal of Psycho-Analysis*, 66, 447–454.

Joseph, B. (1989). *Psychic equilibrium and psychic change*. Routledge.
Joseph, B. (1992). Psychic change: Some perspectives. *International Journal of Psycho-Analysis*, 73, 237–243.
Klein, M. (1921). The development of a child. In M. Klein, *Love, guilt and reparation and other works (1921–1945)* (pp. 1–52). Hogarth Press, 1975.
Klein, M. (1926). The psychological principles of early analysis. In M. Klein, *Love, guilt and reparation and other works, 1921–1945* (pp. 128–138). Hogarth Press, 1975.
Klein, M. (1927). Symposium on child analysis. *International Journal of Psycho-Analysis*, 8, 339–370.
Klein, M. (1930). The importance of symbol-formation in the development of the ego. *International Journal of Psycho-Analysis*, 11, 225–275.
Klein, M. (1932). *The psycho-analysis of children*. Hogarth Press.
Klein, M. (1946). Notes on some schizoid mechanisms. *International Journal of Psycho-Analysis*, 27, 99–110.
Klein, M. (1952). Some theoretical conclusions regarding the emotional life of the infant. In M. Klein, P. Heimann, S. Isaacs, & J. Riviere (Eds.), *Developments in psycho-analysis* (pp. 198–236). Hogarth Press.
Klein, M. (1955). The psycho-analytic play technique: Its history and significance. In M. Klein, *Envy and gratitude and other works* (pp. 122–140). Hogarth Press.
Klein, M. (1961). *Narrative of a child analysis: The conduct of the psycho-analysis of children as seen in the treatment of a ten-year-old boy*. Hogarth Press.
Klein, M. (1975a). *The writings of Melanie Klein* (Vols. 1–4). Hogarth Press.
Klein, M. (1975b). *Love, guilt and reparation and other works 1921–1945* (R. Money-Kyrle, B. Joseph, E. O'Shaughnessy, & H. Segal, Eds.). Hogarth Press [Reprinted by Karnac Books, 1992].
Klein, M. (2017a). *Envy and gratitude and other works 1946–1963* (Routledge Classics ed.). Routledge.
Klein, M. (2017b). *Lectures on technique* (J. Steiner, Ed.). Routledge.
Riviere, J. (1927). Contribution to symposium on child analysis. *International Journal of Psycho-Analysis*, 8, 370–377.
Segal, H. (1964). *Introduction to the work of Melanie Klein*. Heinemann.
Segal, H. (1997). *Psychoanalysis, literature and war: Papers 1972–1995*. Routledge.
Spillius, E. B. (2007). *Encounters with Melanie Klein*. Routledge.
Spillius, E. B., Milton, J., Garvey, P., Couve, C., & Steiner, D. (2011). *The new dictionary of Kleinian thought*. Routledge.
Steiner, J. (2020). *Illusion, disillusion, and irony in psychoanalysis*. Routledge.

Suggested Reading

Garvey, P. (2023). *Melanie Klein: A contemporary introduction.* Routledge.

Chapter 3

Interpretation in Wilfred Bion's Writings

In his seminal paper "Attacks on Linking" (1959), Wilfred Bion provided an unusually candid account of a clinical failure that became foundational for his understanding of psychoanalytic interpretation. In the section entitled "Denial of Normal Degrees of Projective Identification," (312) Bion recounts how a patient attempted to project overwhelming fears of death into him, in the hope that the analyst's mind could contain, modify, and eventually return them in a tolerable form. Instead, Bion realized in hindsight, he had responded with what he calls "routine interpretations"— interventions that carried no emotional presence, offered no true containment, and were thus experienced by the patient as an outright rejection. As Bion writes: "*This patient had had to deal with a mother who could not tolerate such feelings and evacuated them instead*" (Bion, 1959, p. 312, emphasis added). The analytic misstep thus reproduced, rather than transformed, the infantile trauma of an unavailable or unreceiving object.

The clinical consequences of this failure, Bion explains, were dramatic: instead of finding relief through containment, the patient felt that his emotional pain had intensified after being "evacuated" by the analyst. The urgent communication of unbearable psychic states met with an obstruction, and this led the patient to escalate the forcefulness of his projective identifications—pushing more desperately and violently into the analyst in order to be felt and held. For Bion, the crucial distinction was that this escalation was not a destructive attack, though it might have resembled one, but rather a desperate attempt to overcome

DOI: 10.4324/9781003590750-4

the analyst's denial of entry. The true error, Bion insists, lay in his misinterpretation: he had treated the patient's projection as aggression, whereas in fact it signaled an urgent appeal for survival through containment (Bion, 1959, pp. 312–313).

This realization led Bion to reformulate the very nature of interpretation in psychoanalysis. For him, the analyst's specific action is not the delivery of theoretical insight, but *a spoken interpretation at the point of urgency*, following the patient's projection of raw, unbearable anxiety into the analyst. The analyst must wait in a state that abandons expectation, memory, or desire, in order to receive these projected parts of the patient and contain them, rather than defensively rejecting them (Bion, 1992/1967). Only in this receptive stance can the analyst's interpretation function as a true *link*—restoring the patient's capacity to think and to experience continuity of being. In this way, Bion's own clinical failure crystallized his conviction that interpretation is inseparable from containment: to speak effectively at the right moment, the analyst must first suffer, bear, and metabolize the patient's unbearable states, transforming what would otherwise remain destructive evacuations into the beginnings of meaning.

Bion's recognition that interpretation must emerge from containment rather than theoretical knowledge raised a fundamental question: how does the analyst discern, within the chaos of projections and fragmented communications, the precise interpretation that will create meaning? This question led Bion to develop his concept of the "selected fact."

The Selected Fact: The Yearning for Meaning Within Psychic Chaos

When Bion borrowed the concept of the "selected fact" from the mathematician Henri Poincaré, he was not merely engaging in theoretical cross-pollination between disciplines. Rather, he was articulating something fundamental about the human mind's desperate need to find coherence in the face of overwhelming fragmentation—a need that sits at the very heart of both mathematical discovery and psychoanalytic interpretation.

The selected fact, as Bion understood it, emerges from what we might call the epistemological crisis of the paranoid-schizoid position. Here, the mind confronts a landscape of unrelated, scattered elements that resist integration. It is a state familiar to anyone who has sat with a patient whose associations seem to lead nowhere, whose material appears to lack any organizing principle. The analyst, like Poincaré's mathematician confronting disparate mathematical elements, searches for that which might suddenly "introduce order where the appearance of disorder reigned" (Bion, 1962).

Yet Bion's insight was more radical than a simple application of mathematical thinking to psychoanalytic practice. He recognized that the selected fact represents a particular kind of emotional experience—one that combines the exhilaration of creative synthesis with the simultaneous awareness of vast territories that remain uncharted. This is not merely an intellectual exercise but a profoundly emotional encounter with the unknown.

The distinction Bion draws between the selected fact proper and its cousin, interpretation, reveals a subtle but crucial difference in therapeutic function. The selected fact belongs to the realm of discovery—it is something the patient must find for themselves, an internal recognition that precipitates movement from paranoid-schizoid to depressive position. When a patient suddenly grasps a connection between previously disparate aspects of their experience, when meaning crystallizes from apparent chaos, they are experiencing their own selected fact.

Interpretation, however, serves a different master: repair rather than discovery. When the analyst offers an interpretation employing what Bion calls a "definitory hypothesis"—such as the word "breast" applied to material that bears no surface resemblance to its historical meaning—they are providing something the patient cannot yet find for themselves. This is neither patronizing nor premature; it is recognition that sometimes the capacity for discovery itself needs restoration.

The analyst faces a paradox: offering interpretations that function like selected facts while knowing they cannot truly be discoveries the patient makes independently. This "necessary fiction" creates the conditions for genuine discovery to emerge.

Bion's treatment of causality reveals his profound insight into the human tendency to mistake explanatory convenience for truth. Drawing on Hume's insights about constant conjunction, he argues that both cause and selected fact belong to the realm of belief rather than empirical fact. This is a sophisticated understanding of how the mind creates meaning.

The psychotic use of causality demonstrates the pathological extreme of this process. When the patient experiences cause as having "existence as a thing in itself" (Bion, 1992, p. 276), when objects appear to cohere voluntarily and independently of the patient's volition while simultaneously being part of their personality, we witness the mind's desperate attempt to create coherence through omnipotent control. The patient becomes responsible for connections they cannot influence—a position of simultaneous power and helplessness that characterizes much psychotic experience.

For the non-psychotic personality, cause functions as what Bion might call a "useful falsehood"—effective precisely because its limitations are acknowledged. The example of sunrise serves both purposes in his work: sometimes illustrating the utility of false but workable concepts, sometimes demonstrating the damage that occurs when convenient fictions are mistaken for truth. This duality captures something essential about human thinking: both our need for organizing principles and the danger of forgetting their provisional nature.

Bion's distinction between selected fact and cause along temporal lines opens up another dimension of clinical understanding. The selected fact operates in a realm where time is excluded, creating synthesis among elements experienced as contemporaneous. Cause, by contrast, organizes objects scattered in time, imposing sequential narrative on experience.

This temporal distinction shapes analytic technique: selected facts reveal patterns outside linear time, while causality traces developmental sequences across temporal gaps.

Both modes are necessary, but they serve different functions. The timeless realm of the selected fact allows for those moments of insight that seem to illuminate everything at once—sudden recognitions that reorganize entire landscapes of meaning. The temporal realm of causality provides the scaffolding for ongoing understanding, the narrative threads that connect past to present to future.

Bion's work offers both guidance—in tolerating confusion until genuine patterns emerge—and a warning against explanatory systems that provide false certainty instead of genuine understanding.

The analyst working in a Bionian framework learns to distinguish between interpretation that opens and interpretation that closes, between formulations that enhance the patient's capacity for discovery and those that substitute the analyst's understanding for the patient's development. This requires what we might call productive uncertainty—the ability to remain genuinely not-knowing while maintaining therapeutic presence and authority.

This is perhaps Bion's greatest gift to analytic thinking: the recognition that our most sophisticated tools for creating meaning are also our greatest obstacles to encountering truth. The selected fact emerges not through clever interpretation but through the analyst's willingness to be genuinely surprised by what emerges in the space between two minds struggling toward understanding.

Although Bion stopped writing explicitly about the selected fact after 1965, this does not mean he abandoned the concept. The selected fact evolved and developed into the concept of O, which made its debut in "Transformations." The connection between these concepts is profound: the selected fact is present indirectly in his concept of O, and contact with O is really the only way one could possibly intuit the selected fact.

The later emphasis on transformations and invariance maintains the core insight about underlying patterns while shifting attention to the observational process itself (Reiner, 2025).

This progression mirrors the development of any vital concept in psychoanalytic thinking: formulations that are initially helpful but eventually become limiting, requiring new language to capture evolving understanding. The selected fact served Bion well in articulating the relationship between chaos and order in mental life, but his later work needed more flexible tools to explore the infinite complexity of psychic transformation.

Yet the core insight remains: the human mind's capacity to discover coherence in apparent chaos, and the analyst's role in facilitating this discovery through interpretation that repairs rather than merely explains. The selected fact, even in its abandonment, continues to illuminate something essential about how meaning emerges in the analytic encounter.

Reverie and Alpha-Function

The paradox of psychoanalytic interpretation lies not in what it reveals but in how it transforms the very material it seeks to understand. When Bion (1962) proposed that nothing can become conscious without prior unconscious elaboration, he was describing a fundamental architecture of mind that challenges our most basic assumptions about the relationship between experience and understanding.

Bion's extension of Freud's dream theory represents one of the most radical departures from classical psychoanalytic orthodoxy. This reversal of the traditional psychoanalytic formula challenges the directional assumption embedded in Freud's famous dictum "where id was, there ego shall be." Instead, Bion suggests a circular process whereby conscious material must be subjected to dream-work to render it suitable for psychic storage and transformation. The dream is no longer simply the "royal road" to the unconscious but becomes the very mechanism by which reality itself becomes psychically digestible.

The concept of dream-work-α emerged from Bion's clinical observations of patients who seemed unable to dream, yet who desperately needed to engage in dream-like processes during the analytic session itself. These patients, often displaying psychotic features, presented the analyst with a peculiar challenge: they required the analyst to perform the dreaming function that they themselves could not access. Yet Bion recognized the inherent danger in this situation. The analyst must not dream for the patient—such an approach would constitute a form of psychic intrusion that replicates the very projective identification processes that keep the patient imprisoned in their pathology.

This distinction—between dreaming for the patient and dreaming the session—represents one of Bion's most subtle clinical insights. The analyst's reverie must remain genuinely their own while simultaneously providing the containing function that allows the patient's fragmented material to cohere. It is a delicate balance between engagement and separateness, between receptivity and autonomy.

Bion's shift from dream-work-α to alpha-function represented a broader theory: how the mind transforms raw experience (beta elements) into elements suitable for thought and dreaming (alpha elements).

This transformational capacity operates through what Bion identified as maternal reverie. Toward the end of Chapter 12 of *Learning from Experience*, Bion asks: "When a mother loves the infant, what does she do it with?" He replies: "Leaving aside the physical channels of communication my impression is that her love is expressed by reverie" (Bion, 1962). The development of the infant's alpha capacity depends fundamentally on the mother's capacity for reverie, which enables her to receive any psychic object from the infant and submit it to the process of transformation through her own alpha-function.

Parsons (2021) describes reverie as "a way for the analyst to bring into resonance all the levels of awareness of his being" (p. 72) to be available for the patient's experience resulting in an "inner clarity" (p. 72) like the openness of water or sky.

The clinical implications become vivid in Parsons' examination of how the same interpretive content can constitute entirely different interventions depending on the analyst's state of mind. His example of the teacher-patient who could only "let go" when alone illuminates this distinction. An interpretation like "you probably see me as a rival and you are afraid that I will spoil your creativity" (interpretation A) differs fundamentally from "there are two of us in this room" when the latter emerges from the analyst's reverie rather than mechanical application of theoretical knowledge.

The difference, Parsons (2021) demonstrates, lies not in manifest content but in what he calls the point of departure in the psyche of the analyst (p. 75). When the analyst employs alpha-function through reverie, the interpretation must evolve from A to what he terms B2—the same words as the mechanical formulation but emerging from a fundamentally different transformational process. This evolution "can only occur by bringing into play a larger and deeper capacity, namely, the capacity for reverie" (p. 75).

Cassorla's (2008) clinical work with borderline patients reveals how these transformational processes operate in the most challenging therapeutic situations. His observations of "chronic enactments"—those seemingly stagnant periods when analyst and patient appear trapped in unproductive collusions—demonstrate how implicit alpha-function operates below the threshold of conscious awareness. During these periods, "unconscious exchanges occur between the dyad, in which the analyst provides implicit alpha-function to the patient, little by little recovering the traumatized parts" (p. 161).

Chronic enactments serve multiple functions: avoiding trauma revival, using the analyst as protective shield, employing the analyst's alpha-function, and making time for collaborative restoration of injured mental parts.

This understanding illuminates Bion's digestive metaphor for dream-work. Just as the alimentary system breaks down food into forms that can nourish the organism, dream-work processes raw experience into elements that can be stored, combined, and utilized for psychological development. The failure of this digestive function creates what Bion observed in psychotic patients—individuals who seem to have contact with reality but can make remarkably little use of it. They possess the raw material of experience but lack the apparatus to transform it into psychically nutritious elements.

The analyst working with such patients must function as what might be called an auxiliary digestive system, processing the patient's raw communications through their own dream-work apparatus and offering back transformed elements that the patient can potentially incorporate. This is not interpretation in the classical sense but a more fundamental containing and transforming function.

Cassorla's clinical examples (2008) demonstrate how this process unfolds over time. In the case of Patient K., the analyst's eventual "failure"—banging his hand on the chair arm in frustration—paradoxically opened up space for genuine contact. Similarly, with Patient T., the analyst's move to a medical building precipitated what initially appeared to be therapeutic disaster but ultimately allowed traumatic material to surface and become available for processing. These "acute enactments" revealed that apparent therapeutic progress had actually been defensive collusion, while the disruption of this collusion allowed genuine alpha-function to operate (2008, p. 165–167).

The temporal dimensions of these processes reveal something crucial about Bion's understanding of unconscious thinking. His assertion that dream-work operates continuously, not just during sleep, fundamentally alters our understanding of when and how unconscious thinking occurs. The conventional psychoanalytic model assumes a temporal succession from unconscious to conscious, as if mental contents traveled in one direction along a temporal arc.

In this sense, Bion's theory of alpha-function cannot be reduced to a clinical device alone; it carries a profound ontological claim about the very conditions of human thought. The notion of "thoughts without a thinker" suggests that thinking precedes the thinker, that there exists a primordial field of proto-experience in search of psychic form. Dreaming, therefore, is not only a psychological process but also the activity through which experience comes into being as experience—the moment when raw impressions are granted symbolic existence. To dream is to inhabit the very threshold between chaos and form, between what cannot yet be borne and what can become representable.

Bion proposes a simultaneous functioning of conscious and unconscious processes, with conscious material requiring unconscious elaboration before it can become genuinely available to consciousness.

This temporal paradox has profound implications for analytic technique. If the analyst is to work with unconscious processes occurring in the present moment rather than interpreting unconscious material from the past, attention must focus on ongoing transformational processes rather than archaeological excavation. The notion of "thoughts without a thinker" becomes crucial here—meaningful thoughts may exist in the analytic space before either participant consciously recognizes them.

The analyst's anxiety, in this framework, becomes a diagnostic indicator of their refusal to engage in the dreaming process. When the analyst experiences anxiety during a session, it may signal that they are defending against the primary process thinking that would allow them to metabolize the patient's communications. The formula "not (dream) = resist = not (introject)" captures the interconnected nature of these defensive operations (Bion, 1992).

Yet this understanding requires extraordinary preparation on the part of the analyst. Bion's (1992) observation that "the analyst must have plenty of sleep" (p. 120) if they are to dream the session without sleeping reflects his understanding that the analyst's psychological state directly affects their capacity to provide the containing function that analysis requires. This preparation involves maintaining access to unconscious processes through ongoing analysis, developing tolerance for ambiguity and uncertainty, and cultivating what Bion (1965) calls "analytically trained intuition" (p. 18).

Reverie is not gentle fantasy but dwelling within the unbearable—sharing unformed existence while resisting both premature meaning-making and collapse. In this fragile interval, new psychic reality emerges.

The analyst working in a Bionian framework must also develop comfort with being perceived as unreasonable or even mad. The very capacity to engage with primary process material and offer transformations of the patient's communications will often be experienced as disturbing or incomprehensible. The analyst must be "tough and resilient enough to be regarded and treated as insane while being sane" (Bion, 1991).

Bion was acutely aware that emphasis on the analyst's dreaming function could lead to theoretical and clinical excesses. His warning about the dangerous doctrine opening the way for the analyst who theorizes unhampered by the facts of practice reveals his concern that psychoanalytic theory might become detached from clinical reality (Bion, 1965). The safeguards he proposed remain essential: rigorous attention to clinical facts rather than theoretical preconceptions; speaking with minimal ambiguity while recognizing the patient's freedom to receive interpretations as they choose; and acknowledging that formulations represent what the analyst thinks is happening rather than claiming certain knowledge of objective truth.

These considerations reveal the profound ethical dimensions of working with alpha-function. The analyst's capacity to transform beta elements into alpha elements carries enormous responsibility—they become, in effect, co-creators of the patient's psychic reality. This is why the quality of the analyst's reverie, their capacity to maintain authentic engagement with unconscious processes, becomes not merely a technical consideration but a moral imperative.

The emphasis on truth in Bion's work cannot be overstated. His assertion that "healthy mental growth seems to depend on truth as the living organism depends on food" (Bion, 1965, p. 38) places truthfulness at the center of the analytic enterprise. Yet this is not truth as correspondence to external reality but truth as authentic engagement with psychic reality.

For contemporary analysts, these insights require fundamental shifts in understanding both preparation and practice. The analyst's capacity for reverie cannot be reduced to technique but must emerge from sustained cultivation of what Parsons (2021) calls "inner clarity"—that transparency of psychic space that allows for genuine receptiveness to whatever emerges in the analytic encounter.

Cassorla's work with borderline patients illustrates the particular demands (2008) that this places on the analyst. Such patients often "cling to the analyst, using him as a protective shield against reality traumas," requiring the analyst to function as auxiliary alpha-function (174) while gradually recovering the patient's own capacity for symbolization. The analyst must maintain implicit alpha-function even during periods of apparent therapeutic stalemate, slowly injecting transformational capacity through unconscious channels.

This process requires what might be called productive confusion—the analyst's ability to allow meaning to emerge rather than imposing premature understanding. The analyst must develop tolerance for ambiguity while maintaining what Bion calls commitment to truth. This represents one of psychoanalysis's most demanding requirements: remaining open to transformation while preserving observational rigor.

The integration of these insights reveals something profound about the nature of psychoanalytic action. If consciousness depends upon unconscious elaboration, then the analyst's primary function is not interpretation in the classical sense but provision of a transformational environment. The analyst becomes a living demonstration of alpha-function in operation, offering their own capacity for reverie as a model and support for the patient's developing ability to transform raw experience into psychic reality.

This understanding transforms our conception of resistance, transference, and therapeutic action. What appears as resistance may represent the patient's protective efforts to avoid premature exposure to unmetabolized experience. Transference becomes not merely repetition but the patient's attempt to use the analyst's alpha-function to process experiences that remain in beta element form. Therapeutic action occurs not through insight alone but through gradual restoration of the patient's own capacity for alpha-function through sustained exposure to the analyst's transformational processes.

The profound implications extend beyond the consulting room into fundamental questions about mind, reality, and human development. If alpha-function operates through unconscious communication between minds, then the implications for early development, education, and social interaction become immense. The mother's capacity for reverie becomes not merely a nurturing function but a fundamental requirement for the infant's cognitive and emotional development.

This perspective illuminates the particular challenges of working with patients who have experienced early trauma or developmental disruption. Such patients may lack not only the content of secure early relationships but the very apparatus for transforming experience into thinkable form. The analyst's task becomes not interpretation of unconscious content but provision of basic transformational capacity—what Cassorla (2008) calls the "implicit alpha-function" (p. 161) that operates below conscious awareness.

The contemporary relevance of these insights requires a fundamental humility about what analysis can accomplish while simultaneously recognizing its extraordinary potential. The analyst cannot cure patients or provide missing experiences, but they can offer their own alpha-function as a model and support for the patient's developing capacity to transform raw experience into psychic reality. This represents perhaps the most profound form of therapeutic generosity—the offering of one's own mind as a transformational resource for another's development.

The challenge for contemporary psychoanalysis lies in integrating these insights without losing the rigor and precision that Bion himself demanded. The analyst's reverie must remain disciplined by clinical observation and theoretical coherence while preserving the openness to transformation that makes analytic work possible. This remains one of the most demanding and potentially rewarding aspects of psychoanalytic practice—working with processes that cannot be directly perceived but only inferred from their effects, serving as custodians of transformational processes that remain largely mysterious yet fundamentally necessary for human psychological development.

While alpha-function and the selected fact address how meaning emerges from chaos, Bion recognized that some dimensions of analytic experience transcend meaning-making altogether. This led him to develop his most enigmatic concept: O.

The Mystery of O and the Limits of Language in Bionian Interpretation

Perhaps no concept in Bion's work is more central to understanding his approach to interpretation than what he designates simply as "O"—a symbol that represents the ineffable, ultimate reality of the analytic situation. O represents the thing-in-itself of the analytic encounter, the ultimate reality, or "invariance"—the unknowable essence that underlies all psychoanalytic phenomena but can never be directly apprehended (Sandler, 2005, p. 178). Unlike traditional psychoanalytic concepts that seek to make the unconscious conscious, O deliberately preserves mystery as an essential element of human experience. It is not something to be discovered or decoded, but rather approached with what Bion calls "awe" and "reverence"—emotional states that acknowledge the limits of rational understanding while remaining open to transformation.

The clinical implications of orienting toward O rather than knowledge (K) are profound and deserve careful consideration. Traditional interpretation operates within what Bion calls the "Klink"—the domain of knowing, learning, and understanding. The analyst gathers information about the patient's history, observes patterns, applies theoretical frameworks, and offers interpretations designed to increase insight. This approach, while valuable, ultimately remains trapped within the realm of what can be consciously grasped and verbally articulated. There is something deeply familiar about this mode of working—it satisfies our need to understand, to make sense, to feel competent in our professional role. Yet Bion suggests that this very familiarity may be precisely what prevents us from encountering the more elusive dimensions of psychic reality.

The movement from K to O represents more than a technical adjustment; it constitutes a fundamental reorientation of analytic attention. Where K seeks to know about the patient, O requires that we become present with what the patient is becoming. This distinction is not merely philosophical but intensely practical. Consider the difference between saying "You seem angry because your mother didn't validate your needs" and saying "Something fierce is stirring in the room right now." The first interpretation operates within the Klink, connecting present experience to past understanding through causal explanation. The second attempts to stay closer to O, acknowledging the emergence of something that cannot yet be fully grasped or explained.

Bion recognized that words derive from sensuous experience yet must address non-sensuous realities. This creates a paradox: using language to approach what exceeds linguistic capture.

Bion's approach requires a fundamental shift from K to O—from knowing to being. Bion thought that the analyst's concern is not with what can be known about the patient but with what the patient is becoming in the present moment (Bion, 1967) . This orientation demands that the analyst abandon the security of theoretical knowledge and enter what he calls "the unknown territory" (Bion, 2013a, p. 142) of the analytic encounter without predetermined maps or destinations. The analyst must develop what we might call a tolerance for productive confusion—the capacity to remain present with emerging reality without immediately translating it into familiar categories.

This tolerance becomes crucial when we recognize that the limitation of language does not render interpretation futile but places it within a dialectic of saying and unsaying. The analyst's words are valuable not as final truths but as invitations to further exploration, as markers pointing toward experiences that exceed linguistic capture. Every interpretation carries within it an acknowledgment of its own inadequacy, an implicit recognition that something essential always remains beyond the reach of words. This is not a failure of technique but a fundamental condition of human communication when it attempts to engage with the depths of psychic experience.

When an analyst works with a patient struggling with profound depression, they may discover that traditional interpretive language seems to miss the essential quality of the patient's experience. Following Bion's approach, the analyst might begin to speak more tentatively: "It's as if there's a darkness that can't be put into words," or "Something important seems to be happening in the silence." These less saturated interpretations can create space for the patient's own language to emerge, allowing them to approach their experience without the constraint of predetermined meanings. The analyst's reticence becomes not an abdication of interpretive responsibility but a recognition that some forms of psychic pain require a different kind of language—one that honors the unspeakable without rushing to make it speak.

This shift from interpreting about O to allowing O to manifest through the analytic process represents perhaps the most challenging aspect of Bion's contribution to psychoanalytic practice. It requires what he calls "becoming O" rather than knowing about O—a transformation in the analyst's state of being that creates conditions for genuine encounter with psychological reality. This is not a technique that can be taught through instruction but a capacity that must be cultivated through discipline—the systematic suspension of memory, desire, and understanding in favor of presence with the immediate, evolving truth of the analytic situation.

The concept of O also illuminates why Bion insists that the most important truths in analysis cannot be communicated directly through interpretation. O exists in the realm of experience rather than knowledge, in the space between words rather than in their explicit content. This understanding leads us to examine one of Bion's most profound concepts: atonement, or at-one-ment. The hyphenated spelling is deliberate, emphasizing not religious expiation but a state of being at one with ultimate reality. As Bion wrote, "The central postulate is that atonement with ultimate reality, or O, as I have called it to avoid involvement with existing associations, is essential to harmonious mental growth" (Bion, 1967, p. 145).

The notion of at-one-ment suggests something quite different from traditional psychoanalytic goals of insight or understanding. Rather than achieving knowledge about unconscious conflicts or developmental failures, the analytic process seeks to achieve a state of being that harmonizes with reality as it actually is, rather than as we wish it to be or fear it might be. This harmonization cannot be forced or manufactured through interpretive cleverness; it emerges through what Bion describes as a particular quality of attention that neither grasps nor rejects what is present.

Reality cannot be known but must be "been"—like potatoes that can be grown or eaten but not sung. The analyst must shift from knowing about the patient's reality to being with it.

This grammatical innovation—the suggestion that reality requires "being" rather than knowing—points toward something essential about the quality of presence that effective analysis requires. The analyst cannot stand outside the patient's experience and comment upon it from a position of objective knowledge. Instead, the analyst must find ways of participating in the emergence of the patient's reality while maintaining enough separateness to offer a useful perspective. This is a delicate balance that requires constant adjustment and cannot be reduced to technical rules or procedures.

The clinical implications become clear when Bion states that "the interpretation is an actual event in an evolution of O that is common to analyst and analysand" (Bion, 1970, p. 27). This transforms our understanding of what happens when we speak in the consulting room. The interpretation does not describe or explain reality—it participates in reality's evolution. It is not a statement about truth but an enactment of truth's emergence. This is why Bion insists that "formulations of the events of analysis made in the course of analysis must possess value different from that of formulations made extra-sessionally" (p. 26). The living interpretation, offered in the heat of the analytic moment, conducts transformation in O rather than mere knowledge about O.

This distinction helps to explain why interpretations that seem theoretically correct can fall completely flat, while others that emerge spontaneously from the analyst's state of at-one-ment can transform both participants. The difference lies not in the content of the words but in the quality of being from which they emerge. An interpretation that arises from genuine contact with O carries something that cannot be manufactured through theoretical understanding or technical skill alone. It partakes of the reality it seeks to address rather than merely commenting upon it from the outside.

The analyst who achieves this state discovers that "in so far as the analyst becomes O he is able to know the events that are evolutions of O" (Bion, 1970, p. 27). But this "becoming" requires a particular discipline—what Bion calls faith, "faith that there is an ultimate reality and truth—the unknown, unknowable, 'formless infinite'" (p. 31). This is not faith in any particular truth or theory, but faith in the existence of truth itself, and in its capacity to emerge through the analytic process. Such faith requires the analyst to relinquish the security of knowing in advance what the patient needs or what the session should accomplish.

The paradox is that achieving at-one-ment requires tolerating profound not-knowing. As Bion observed, drawing on the mystic tradition, those who have contacted O must develop a capacity to tolerate paradoxes. The analyst must be prepared, as Wordsworth wrote of poetry, to recollect the experience in tranquility and discern it as part of a greater whole. But—and here Bion adds his characteristic note of warning—"the discoverer must be prepared to find that he has started another round of group oscillations. Persecution↔Depression" (Bion, 1997, p. 285). Each moment of at-one-ment, each genuine interpretation, disrupts the existing order and initiates new cycles of confusion and clarity.

This cycling between persecution and depression reflects something fundamental about the nature of psychological growth. Genuine contact with reality, whether in analysis or elsewhere, tends to disturb established patterns of thought and feeling. What felt familiar and secure suddenly appears questionable; what seemed certain reveals itself as provisional. The patient who achieves a moment of genuine self-recognition may immediately feel persecuted by this new awareness or depressed by its implications. The analyst who offers an interpretation that truly connects with O may find themselves doubting everything they thought they knew about the patient or about analysis itself.

Working at these edges of linguistic possibility demands that analysts develop what might be called interpretive restraint—the capacity to offer words that acknowledge their own limitations while creating space for the emergence of meaning that exceeds language. This approach recognizes that the most profound therapeutic moments often occur in the spaces between words, in the silences where something ineffable passes between analyst and patient. The challenge is to speak in ways that honor both the necessity of language and its fundamental inadequacy to capture the depths of human experience.

This interpretive restraint requires a particular kind of discipline from the analyst. Rather than rushing to fill silences with understanding or to resolve confusion with explanation, the analyst must learn to tolerate states of not-knowing that may feel professionally uncomfortable. The analyst must develop what Keats calls "negative capability"—the capacity to remain in uncertainty and doubt rather than irritably reaching after fact and reason. As Bion (1970) writes "When a man is capable of being in uncertainties, mysteries, doubts, without any irritable reaching after fact and reason" (125). This does not mean abandoning all theoretical knowledge or clinical judgment, but rather holding these tools lightly, ready to set them aside when they become obstacles to genuine encounter.

The implications extend beyond individual technique to fundamental questions about the nature and purpose of psychoanalytic treatment. If the goal is at-one-ment with O rather than the acquisition of insight about unconscious conflicts, then the criteria for successful analysis must shift accordingly. Progress cannot be measured simply in terms of symptom reduction or increased self-understanding, though these may certainly occur. Instead, the analyst must attend to subtler indicators: the patient's growing capacity to tolerate uncertainty, their increasing ability to remain present with difficult emotions, their developing faith in the possibility of truth beyond immediate understanding.

This reorientation places new demands on analytic training and supervision. Future analysts must learn not only how to interpret but how to refrain from interpreting when interpretation would interrupt the emergence of O. They must develop tolerance for states of confusion and not-knowing that traditional training may have taught them to avoid. Most importantly, they must cultivate their own capacity for at-one-ment through personal analysis that goes beyond symptom resolution to contact with their own ultimate reality.

The challenge for contemporary psychoanalysis is to maintain this delicate balance between saying and unsaying, between the necessity of language and the recognition of its fundamental inadequacy to capture the depths of human experience. In this light, Bion's concept of O stands not as a mystical abstraction but as a practical recognition of the limits within which all genuine interpretive work must operate. It reminds us that the most important aspects of human experience may be precisely those that resist direct communication, requiring instead a quality of presence that allows truth to emerge in its own time and in its own way.

Bion's radical reconceptualization of interpretation has been taken even further by contemporary analysts who have transformed his insights into new clinical methodologies. Among the most innovative are Antonino Ferro and Giuseppe Civitarese, who have developed Bion's concepts into what they call "Bionian Field Theory" (BFT).

The Art of Not-Knowing: Ferro and Civitarese on Interpretation as Creative Transformation

If Bion taught analysts to approach each session without memory and desire, Antonino Ferro and Giuseppe Civitarese have developed this principle into a sophisticated clinical methodology that fundamentally transforms interpretation from archaeological excavation into creative co-construction. Their work represents perhaps the most radical extension of Bion's late thinking, pushing his concepts of O and at-one-ment into new territories of clinical practice that challenge traditional notions of analytic authority and technique.

Ferro's Theoretical Foundation

Ferro's approach begins with a fundamental reconceptualization of how analysts should understand patient communications. Rather than viewing them as coded messages about past trauma or internal phantasies requiring decoding, he conceptualizes them as narrative derivatives of alpha elements—real-time pictographs of the emotional experience unfolding within what he terms the analytic field (Ferro, 2002c). This theoretical shift means that every story a patient tells, whether about mundane daily events or significant relationships, serves as a vehicle for communicating the immediate emotional truth of the analytic moment rather than historical material requiring interpretation.

Ferro developed the Barangers' bipersonal field into a multi-personal framework, focusing on "functional aggregates"—affective holograms jointly constructed by patient and analyst in a shared mental space where meaning is co-created rather than discovered.

The clinical implications of this theoretical foundation are profound. When Ferro worked with Marcella, a fifteen-year-old patient who complained about inadequate school facilities, his response demonstrated this principle in action. Rather than interpreting her concerns as symbolic communications about her internal world or the analytic relationship, he responded to the manifest content with what he terms an unsaturated interpretation, preserving space for new meaning to emerge (Ferro, 2002c, p. 185). This technical approach reflects his belief that premature interpretive closure—what he describes as attempts to reveal true truth—functions as a form of intellectual violence that forecloses possibility rather than opening it (Ferro, 2006b, p. 1).

The Evolution Toward Dream-Work

Ferro's theoretical development was significantly influenced by his deepening engagement with Bion's concepts of alpha-function and dream-work. Drawing on Bion's understanding that thinking itself emerges from the transformation of raw emotional experience (beta elements) into thinkable thoughts (alpha elements), Ferro reconceptualized the analytic process as fundamentally concerned with enhancing the patient's capacity for psychological digestion and dream-work (Ferro & Nicoli, 2023). This shift moved his approach away from interpretation as explanation toward what he calls transformative interpretation—interventions that actively facilitate the transformation of both participants in the analytic encounter.

Central to this evolution was Ferro's collaboration with American analysts, particularly Howard Levine and James Grotstein, who helped to bridge his field concepts with Bionian dream theory. This cross-pollination led to what Otto Kernberg designated as Bion Field Theory, distinguishing it from other field approaches through its emphasis on the dreamlike functioning of minds and the gradual generation of enhanced capacity for psychological transformation (Ferro & Nicoli, 2023). The analyst's role in this framework shifts from that of an interpreting authority to what Ferro describes as a breathing center that must constantly modulate the breaths of the field according to necessity.

Civitarese and the Democracy of Dreaming

Giuseppe Civitarese extends Ferro's work in directions that further challenge traditional analytic hierarchies. Where Ferro focuses on unsaturated interpretation and character development,

Civitarese proposes that interpretation is fundamentally about dreaming together within the analytic field (Civitarese, 2023). This represents a radical reconceptualization: rather than viewing the unconscious as buried material waiting to be excavated, Civitarese suggests it comes into being through the very act of mutual dreaming, with interpretation serving as another form of dream-work rather than its explanation.

Civitarese's contribution centers on his concept of the analytic field as a third space—neither belonging to patient nor analyst but emerging from their interaction in ways that neither can fully control or possess. This space operates according to what he calls field-listening, an attunement not to what the patient really means but to what emerges between the participants (Civitarese, 2023). In this framework, the most significant interpretations may not be verbal at all but might manifest as shared silences, bodily sensations that pass between participants, or mutual experiences of forgetting that reveal more than remembering.

Technical Implications and Clinical Method

The technical approach that emerges from this theoretical framework requires what both theorists describe as a fundamental shift in analytic attitude. Rather than maintaining a position of knowing, the analyst must cultivate the willingness to dwell in uncertainty without irritably reaching after fact and reason (Civitarese, 2023, p. 21). This requires not only tolerance for not-knowing but active faith that the analytic couple, stumbling together in the dark, might create illumination through their very stumbling.

Both Ferro and Civitarese emphasize that this approach demands rigorous attention to the analyst's own mental processes. The analyst's reverie becomes not a distraction from the work but its very essence—the medium through which beta elements are transformed into alpha elements that can be thought and dreamed (Ferro & Di Donna, 2005, p. 93). This places enormous demands on the analyst's capacity for self-reflection and emotional availability while maintaining what Ferro calls a little piece of analytic function that preserves the therapeutic frame.

Ethical and Philosophical Dimensions

Perhaps most significantly, both theorists are making what amounts to an ethical argument disguised as a technical one. They suggest that the traditional interpretive stance—the analyst who knows confronts the patient who doesn't know—not only proves clinically ineffective but potentially recreates the very power dynamics and submissions that brought the patient to analysis initially. Their alternative offers a model of interpretation as mutual vulnerability, whereby the analyst must risk not knowing, risk being changed by the encounter, and risk discovering that carefully cultivated theoretical frameworks might prove inadequate in the face of this particular person's suffering.

This ethical dimension extends to their understanding of therapeutic action itself. Rather than seeking insight as the primary goal, they aim for what Civitarese describes as the development of capacity—the enhanced ability to generate new stories, new connections, and new ways of being alive to one's own experience. Civitarese emphasizes that successful interpretation does not install truth, but rather nurtures conditions for further dreaming (Civitarese, 2023, p. 26). The most effective interpretations, in this view, are often those that interpret nothing directly but instead create conditions for new meanings to emerge.

The vision of interpretation that emerges from Ferro and Civitarese's work represents interpretation as creative art rather than scientific technique. Like musicians who have mastered their instruments but must transcend technique in the moment of performance, the analyst must be simultaneously prepared and unprepared, knowing and unknowing, holding theoretical understanding while remaining open to transformation. Their contribution suggests that in the space between two people courageous enough to not-know together, something genuinely novel can emerge—not discovered or recovered, but created anew during each encounter between two particular individuals willing to dream together.

Conclusion: Interpretation as Faith

Bion's reconceptualization of interpretation represents more than a modification of psychoanalytic technique—it amounts to a complete reimagining of what analytic work can accomplish. By shifting from content-deciphering to truth-orientation, he transformed interpretation from a technical skill into an ethical practice demanding the analyst's full presence. As he concluded in his Los Angeles seminars, "I think that it's a good thing to bet on that if you listen enough, after a time, something evolves. Something pushes out towards you, you begin to notice it, and then an interpretation will come with it" (Bion, 2013a, p. 10–11).

This transformation requires interpretive faith—trusting the analytic process despite uncertainty, and abandoning theoretical security for direct encounter with the unknown.

The revolution that Bion initiated continues to unfold in contemporary psychoanalytic practice. His emphasis on authentic encounter creates bridges between classical and relational approaches without abandoning rigorous attention to unconscious process. Perhaps most significantly, his work suggests that the future of psychoanalytic interpretation lies not in developing increasingly sophisticated theoretical frameworks but in cultivating the analyst's capacity for negative capability—the ability to remain present with uncertainty while trusting in the emergence of meaning from authentic engagement.

In Bion's vision, the analyst doesn't apply psychoanalysis but becomes psychoanalysis through disciplined attention to the unfolding truth of the analytic encounter. This framework transforms interpretation from technical act to ethical stance, whereby the pursuit of emotional truth takes precedence over therapeutic ambition. The most profound interpretive interventions are those that create space for the unknown to emerge rather than foreclosing mystery through premature understanding, making interpretation an act of faith in the human capacity for transformation through authentic encounter with psychological reality.

References

Bion, W. R. (1959). Attacks on linking. *International Journal of Psychoanalysis*, 40, 308–315.

Bion, W. R. (1962). *Learning from experience.* Karnac Books.

Bion, W. R. (1965). *Transformations.* Heinemann Medical Books. (Reprinted by Karnac Books).

Bion, W. R. (1967). *Second thoughts.* Heinemann Medical Books. (Reprinted by Karnac Books).

Bion, W. R. (1970). *Attention and interpretation: A scientific approach to insight in psychoanalysis and groups.* Tavistock Publications. (Reprinted by Karnac Books).

Bion, W. R. (1991). *A memoir of the future.* Karnac Books.

Bion, W. R. (1992). Notes on memory and desire. *Psychoanalytic Forum, 2*, 272. (Original work published 1967)

Bion, W. R. (1992). *Cogitations* (F. Bion, Ed.). Karnac Books.

Bion, W. R. (1997). *Taming wild thoughts.* Karnac Books.

Bion, W. R. (2013a). *Los Angeles seminars and supervision* (J. Aguayo & B. D. Malin, Eds.). Routledge.

Bion, W. R. (2013b). *The complete works of W. R. Bion* (Vol. 16). Karnac Books.

Cassorla, R. M. (2008). The analyst's implicit alpha-function, trauma and enactment in the analysis of borderline patients. *International Journal of Psychoanalysis*, 89(1), 161–180.

Civitarese, G. (2023). *The analytic field and its transformations.* Routledge.

Etchegoyen, R. H. (1991). *The fundamentals of psychoanalytic technique.* Karnac Books.

Ferro, A. (1999). *The bi-personal field.* Routledge.

Ferro, A. (2002a). *In the analyst's consulting room.* Brunner-Routledge.

Ferro, A. (2002b). *Seeds of illness, seeds of recovery: The genesis of suffering and the role of psychoanalysis.* Brunner-Routledge.

Ferro, A. (2002c). Narrative derivatives of alpha elements: Clinical implications. *International Forum of Psychoanalysis*, 11(3), 184–187. doi:10.1080/080370602321021774.

Ferro, A. (2006a). *Psychoanalysis as therapy and storytelling*. Routledge.

Ferro, A. (2006b). Clinical implications of Bion's thought. *International Journal of Psychoanalysis*, 87(4), 989–1003. doi:10.1516/29WN-CXRF-L2QY-4U8J.

Ferro, A., & Di Donna, L. (2005). Conversations with clinicians: Antonino Ferro, M.D. *Fort Da*, 11(1), 92–98.

Ferro, A., & Nicoli, L. (2023). Origins and destinies of the Bion field theory. *International Forum of Psychoanalysis*, 32(3), 153–163. doi:10.1080/0803706X.2022.2091347.

Parsons, M. (2021). Reverie and alpha function. In *Psychoanalysts in session: Clinical glossary of contemporary psychoanalysis*. Routledge.

Sandler, P. C. (2005). *The language of Bion: A dictionary of concepts*. Karnac Books.

Suggested Reading

Reiner, A. (2023). *W. R. Bion's theories of mind: A contemporary introduction*. Routledge.

Chapter 4

Interpretation in Donald Winnicott's Writings

From Truth-Seeking to Trauma Healing: Winnicott's Revolutionary Departure from Classical Psychoanalysis

When Sándor Ferenczi's approach—which held that the therapeutic essence of psychoanalysis resided in profound emotional attunement rather than intellectual interpretation—was forcefully marginalized by Freud and his circle, the field crystallized around a singular conviction: that interpretation yielding insight constituted the paramount curative force. Yet, as with all pendulums swung too far in one direction, the inevitable countermovement was destined to emerge.

How fortunate for the evolution of psychoanalytic thought that the figure who would shepherd this transformation was Donald Winnicott, a clinician whose rare amalgam of qualities—penetrating clinical intuition, imaginative theoretical sophistication, and profound intellectual humility—rendered him uniquely suited to articulate what had been silently gestating in the consulting rooms of countless analysts. His contribution was not merely to offer an alternative, but to weave a tapestry of understanding that honored both the interpretive tradition and the relational depths that Ferenczi had glimpsed.

Winnicott had the rare ability to remain deeply attentive to the patient's subjective experience without imposing theoretical constructs too forcefully. His appreciation for the subtleties of early emotional life, his innovative concepts such as the "holding

DOI: 10.4324/9781003590750-5

environment," and his refusal to be seduced by grand systems allowed psychoanalysis to rediscover its human and relational roots. Unlike more polemical or systematic thinkers, Winnicott encouraged openness, playfulness, and respect for the complexity of human development—qualities that ensured that the new psychoanalytic paradigm would be as compassionate as it is profound. His emphasis on authentic emotional connection, and his willingness to trust the patient's own process, helped psychoanalysis to remain relevant and life-giving to future generations.

Winnicott quietly dismantled the entire edifice of psychoanalytic authority while appearing to do nothing more than pay closer attention to what mothers actually do. His revolution came disguised as common sense, which may be why it took so long for the field to recognize how thoroughly he had transformed the nature of therapeutic action itself.

The history of psychoanalysis reveals two competing traditions for the therapeutic encounter, each carrying profound implications for how we understand healing, knowledge, and human relationship. The first, the *truth-seeking tradition*, stretching from Freud through Klein and early Bion, imagined the analyst as scientist and the patient as research subject—a dyad engaged in the methodical excavation of psychical truth. Here, symptoms were clues, dreams were encrypted messages, and the analyst's interpretive acumen was the primary instrument of cure.

In this classical framework, pathology was understood primarily as the consequence of disavowal—the patient's systematic refusal to acknowledge their inner truth. People preferred to live in illusions, constructing elaborate defensive narratives rather than confronting the reality of their desires, aggression, and vulnerability. Most crucially, they projected unwanted aspects of themselves onto others, unable or unwilling to claim ownership of these disavowed parts. The therapeutic task was therefore one of reclamation: helping patients to recognize and reintegrate what they had expelled from conscious awareness. Healing meant knowing oneself—not in some abstract philosophical sense, but in the concrete recognition of the specific truths one had been hiding from consciousness.

Freud's (1917) characteristic advice to the neurotic patient captures this epistemological faith perfectly: "The guilt … It is in you ... look inward, look into your own depths, learn first and foremost to know yourself!" (pp. 142–143). Knowledge, in this view, is inherently curative. The patient suffers not from what they don't have but from what they won't see. The analyst's role is to illuminate these hidden truths through interpretation, gradually dismantling the patient's defensive structures until they can tolerate knowing what they have always unconsciously known.

The second metaphor, *the trauma healing tradition* which Winnicott developed with characteristic subtlety, reconceived the therapeutic relationship as fundamentally like that between parent and infant. Here, healing occurs not through the acquisition of knowledge but through the provision of a particular kind of relational environment.

What makes this transformation so intriguing is how it emerged from Winnicott's profound skepticism about the very enterprise that had made psychoanalysis famous. Where Freud had proclaimed that neurosis resulted from repressed truth, and Klein had argued with Hannah Segal (1962) that "the goal of the analyst is solely to obtain knowledge and to convey it" (p. 212), Winnicott took a different approach. He used the model of preverbal mother-infant communication as the foundation for understanding the analytic relationship, which consequently redefined the role that interpretation plays in psychoanalytic therapy. This seemingly modest observation contains a revolutionary implication—if the patient already possesses what they need to know, then what exactly is the analyst's function?

Winnicott's answer involves a complete reconceptualization of interpretive authority. Winnicott emphasizes that it is crucial for the analyst to avoid knowing the answers in advance, except when the patient has regressed to the earliest infancy. "I never use long sentences unless I am very tired" (Winnicott, 1965b, p. 167). The analyst should only understand what the patient reveals through their own clues. Winnicott suggests that the goal is not merely to provide assurance but to allow the patient to find and come to terms with the therapeutic object.

Winnicott, more than any of his contemporaries in the United Kingdom, frequently explored the use of prolonged analytic sessions, deliberately creating a space where patients were encouraged to regress. This practice was widely recognized among his colleagues at the time. Often, he and his patient would plan these extended sessions several months ahead, knowing that such an approach could help the patient to hold off an impending psychological breakdown (Bollas, 2013).

The implications of this shift extend to the very goal of treatment. The truth-seeking tradition aims to return disavowed parts of the self through interpretation and insight, helping patients to reclaim projected aspects of their personality and achieve greater integration through understanding. The trauma healing tradition, by contrast, seeks to facilitate what Winnicott (1954) called "going-on-being," that is, the basic continuity of existence that environmental failure can shatter. The goal is not primarily self-knowledge but the capacity for authentic living and creative engagement with reality.

Perhaps nowhere is this difference more evident than in each tradition's understanding of transference. The truth-seeking tradition expects and encourages the development of intense transference reactions that can be interpreted and worked through. The analyst's willingness to function as a "bad object"—to receive and survive the patient's negative projections—is seen as essential to therapeutic progress. The trauma healing tradition, while not avoiding negative transference, does not require it as a necessary phase of treatment.

Yet this neat distinction between truth-seeking and trauma healing contains its own complications. Critics from each camp rightly argue that the dichotomy creates false polarizations. Truth-seeking analysts contend that they too heal trauma, pointing out that their interpretive work addresses the psychological wounds created by early object relationships and constitutional vulnerabilities. Trauma healing practitioners argue that their relational approach inevitably uncovers important truths about the patient's psychological development. The question becomes not whether truth emerges in treatment, but what kind of truth and by what means.

Nevertheless, this distinction remains crucial, and when one reads the case studies of Klein's followers versus those of Winnicott's disciples, the difference is striking: the former approach the patient's communications with suspicion, searching for hidden meanings, while the latter believe and validate the patient's experience; the former carefully avoid any display of reassurance or comfort, while the latter embrace, contain, and hold; the former interpret aggression behind apparent gratitude, while the latter celebrate genuine connection; the former maintain strict boundaries, while the latter adapt the frame to meet developmental needs—creating two fundamentally different therapeutic cultures that, despite theoretical convergences, continue to shape divergent clinical practices.

Winnicott argued that what truly matters to the patient is the analyst's genuine desire to be helpful, their ability to empathetically connect with the patient, their belief in what the patient requires, and their readiness to respond to those needs as soon as they are communicated through verbal, non-verbal, or preverbal means (Winnicott, 1965a).

Language and the Limits of Interpretation: Winnicott's Revolutionary Departure from the Talking Cure

If Winnicott's challenge to psychoanalytic authority was conducted with characteristic indirection, his skepticism about language itself was even more subtle—and perhaps more subversive. In a field that had staked its reputation on being a "talking cure," Winnicott quietly but persistently questioned whether the most significant therapeutic transformations could be captured solely in words. Adam Phillips devotes an extensive discussion to this aspect (Phillips, 1988).

Winnicott gave central importance to the body as the foundation for the development of the psyche—an approach that sets him apart from the psychoanalytic mainstream. While traditional psychoanalysis certainly acknowledged the body in psychic development, it generally treated the body as a locus for meaning—whether as the site of unconscious conflict expressed in conversion symptoms, as a container for instinctual drives, or as the substrate for psychosomatic manifestations and unconscious fantasy. Winnicott, in contrast, emphasized the body as a lived reality, one that cannot be separated from the psyche during the earliest phases of development.

In his essay "Mind and its Relation to the Psyche-Soma" (1954), Winnicott described how, at the beginning of life, there is simply the body—and that any distinction between psyche and soma is a matter of perspective. The development of imagination around bodily sensations, parts, and functions is, for him, the starting point of the psyche. The intricate interplay between psyche and soma constitutes a foundational stage of individual development. Even in later stages—once the experience of the "live body" as something differentiated from the outside world is established—it remains at the core of the imaginative self.

Discussing the process of personalization, one of the pillars of early psychic development in his theory, Winnicott argued that there is no essential identity between self and body at the start of life, but that for health, such integration must eventually be achieved. Gradually, the psyche "comes to terms" with the body, forming a state in which bodily boundaries are experienced as psychic boundaries—a developmental achievement that supports the capacity to experience oneself in the first person. Winnicott acknowledged that not everyone attains this level of integration, and some lose it in the course of life. What makes personalization possible is precisely this process of the psyche grounding itself in the lived experience of the body, with all its sensations and functions, eventually leading to an embodied sense of self.

It's as if the most important truths resist clear articulation and require the kind of hesitant, provisional language that permits multiple meanings to coexist, just as the earliest phase of life involves a fluidity between body and mind before language imposes rigid distinctions.

This seemingly simple observation carries revolutionary implications for therapeutic practice. If human development begins in a fundamentally preverbal realm, and if the most crucial experiences of presence or lack of presence occur before symbolic representation is possible, then what exactly can interpretation accomplish?

Phillips (1988) identifies the central paradox with characteristic clarity: "Can that which is experienced pre-reflectively, in the body but without language, be reached through language?" (p. 133).

The question of how psychological disturbance manifests in bodily symptoms reveals itself to be far more complex than a simple mind-body relationship. Winnicott's clinical observations led him to a counterintuitive insight: what we call psychosomatic illness is not actually about the connection between psyche and soma, but rather about their radical disconnection. The hyphen in "psycho-somatic" does not merely join two aspects of human functioning—it represents a defensive split that keeps them rigidly apart.

This understanding emerges most clearly when we examine how certain patients organize their relationship to medical care itself. Rather than seeking integrated treatment, they seem compelled to scatter their care across multiple providers, each addressing only one fragment of their experience. In his paper "Psycho-somatic Illness in Its Positive and Negative Aspects" (1966), Winnicott described how he treated a young woman with severe anorexia nervosa. What makes this case particularly illuminating is how the therapeutic process eventually facilitated integration. For years, the patient's communications centered exclusively on somatic experiences—belly pains, sensations of objects falling from her body, sharp-edged filing cabinets causing acute physical distress. These could not be interpreted as psychological material or internal objects because they existed precisely in the realm of bodily experience, split off from mental life. The analyst's role during this phase was not to interpret but to survive—to provide an environment within which such primitive communications could be sustained without forcing premature integration.

The crucial moment came when the patient reported a headache. This seemingly minor shift represented a fundamental therapeutic breakthrough, for a headache could be accepted as associated with mental confusion rather than purely somatic disturbance. As Winnicott (1966) noted, "I now interpreted that she was telling me about an illness of her mind, and I therefore slipped over from being part of a psycho-somatic team into the role of psychotherapist" (p. 512). Only then did the belly symptoms disappear, replaced by material that could be worked with psychoanalytically.

This clinical vignette reveals something profound about the nature of interpretation in such cases. During the dissociated phase, the traditional interpretive technique would have been not merely useless but actively harmful. The patient's defensive organization depended precisely on keeping somatic experience separate from psychological meaning. Any attempt to translate bodily symptoms into emotional language would have constituted what Winnicott called "impingement"—an environmental failure that reproduces the original trauma.

This understanding transforms our conception of what interpretation accomplishes in such cases. Interpretation serves an integrative function, helping to heal the split between psyche and soma that constitutes the true illness. The content of interpretation becomes less important than its capacity to demonstrate that psychological and physical experience can coexist within a single therapeutic relationship.

Bonaminio (2012) also illuminates this through Winnicott's radical insight: "I think I interpret mainly to let the patient know the limits of my understanding" (Winnicott, 1963, p. 189). This transforms interpretation from omnipotent knowing to humble recognition of boundaries. The analyst's incomplete understanding becomes, paradoxically, the very thing that enables authentic contact.

This concern about analytic omniscience led Winnicott to develop what might seem like a deliberately imperfect interpretive technique. He notes, with characteristic playfulness, that he interprets because "if I make none the patient gets the impression that I understand everything. In other words, I retain some outside quality by not being quite on the mark—or even by being wrong" (Winnicott, 1969, p. 718). This willingness to be imperfect, even deliberately so, serves a crucial developmental function. It preserves the patient's sense of having a separate mind while still providing the experience of being understood.

This restraint connects to Winnicott's broader understanding of play as the fundamental therapeutic activity. The insight that "the opposite of play is not work but coercion" (Phillips, 1988,

p. 138) transforms how we understand interpretive intervention. Language, when used interpretively, can easily become coercive—imposing meaning rather than facilitating discovery. This danger is particularly acute given the inherent power differential in the analytic situation.

Winnicott's solution involves reconceptualizing interpretation as an element within play rather than an authoritative pronouncement about it. Communication takes place in what he calls the "transitional space between analyst and patient" (Phillips, 1988, p. 138)—a shared area of creative possibility where meanings can emerge collaboratively rather than being imposed by interpretive authority.

This philosophy finds its most radical expression in Winnicott's willingness to withdraw interpretations that don't work. In "The Use of an Object" (Winnicott, 1971a), he writes: "The analyst feels like interpreting, but this can spoil the process, and for the patient can seem like a kind of self-defence" (p. 92).

Winnicott thought that the analyst should "wait" to see how the patient was responding to being in the analytic situation. This was founded on his belief that it was only the patient who had the answers.

Winnicott acknowledges that sometimes patient resistance indicates that he has offered a correct interpretation which the patient is denying. However, he maintains that when an interpretation fails to be effective, it invariably means that he delivered it at an inappropriate time or in an unsuitable manner, and he withdraws it completely without conditions. Even when the content of an interpretation may be accurate, the timing or approach of verbalizing that material could be wrong for that specific moment.

Winnicott (1971a) argues that dogmatic interpretations place children in an impossible position where they must either accept what the analyst says as mere propaganda or reject both the interpretation and the entire therapeutic relationship. He believes it is essential that children feel they have the legitimate right to refuse what he says or how he approaches their material.

This bodily emphasis finds clinical expression in what Bonaminio (2012) calls Winnicott's capacity for "musing" rather than interpreting. The analyst described by Winnicott is, as Bonaminio notes, "someone whom we see simply breathing more than anything else" (p. 1478). This breathing presence, this psychosomatic integrity, becomes more therapeutically significant than mental interpretive activity.

By questioning language's capacity to reach the deepest levels of human experience, Winnicott opened up space for therapeutic approaches that prioritize being over knowing, relationship over insight, and environmental provision over interpretive revelation. The talking cure, in his hands, becomes something more like a "being cure"—a therapeutic encounter in which healing occurs through the quality of presence and relationship rather than through the acquisition of verbal understanding. The paradox is that by talking less about what matters most, we might finally create space for it to emerge.

The Art of Clinical Discrimination: When Analysis Becomes Something Else

What makes a clinician decide that the familiar tools of psychoanalysis might actually harm rather than help? This question haunted Winnicott throughout his career, leading him to develop what might be called a diagnostic sensitivity for the limits of interpretive work itself. His answer was neither theoretical nor ideological but profoundly practical: some patients require something other than interpretive work precisely because their developmental arrests occurred before symbolic thinking became possible.

Winnicott identified five specific conditions that signal the need for what he diplomatically called "something else": where fear of madness dominates the clinical picture; where a successful false self has created a facade that analysis would necessarily destroy; where antisocial tendencies reflect the legacy of deprivation rather than conflict; where inner psychic reality remains unlinked to external experience; and where an ill parental figure continues to dominate the patient's internal world (Winnicott, 1965c).

These are not diagnostic categories in any conventional sense, but rather clinical recognitions of developmental predicaments that interpretation cannot reach. Each represents a different form of environmental failure that occurred before the patient possessed the psychological equipment to process trauma symbolically. For such patients, the analyst's interpretive expertise becomes irrelevant—not because interpretation is wrong, but because it addresses psychological capacities that never had the chance to develop.

This discrimination reveals something crucial about Winnicott's understanding of therapeutic action. Where classical analysis assumes that all patients possess the basic psychological structure necessary for interpretive work—an observing ego, the capacity for symbolic thought, some degree of integration between psyche and soma—Winnicott recognized that environmental failure can interrupt these developmental achievements before they solidify. The analyst's task becomes not interpretation but the provision of conditions within which such basic psychological equipment might finally develop.

What emerges is a picture of psychoanalytic work organized around developmental necessity rather than theoretical consistency. The analyst must diagnose not merely what is unconscious but what is developmentally possible, adjusting technique not to theoretical preference but to the patient's actual psychological capacities. This requires a different kind of clinical listening—to symbolic meaning, developmental arrest, and missing psychological functions.

The Paradox of Psychological Birth: Creating What Was Always There

Perhaps nowhere is Winnicott's departure from classical thinking more evident than in his understanding of how psychological life begins. Where traditional psychoanalysis starts with conflict—the inevitable clash between desire and reality, between id and superego—Winnicott begins with paradox. As Abram (2012) notes, this centers on what Winnicott called "the essential paradox": the object that the infant finds was created by the infant, yet existed all along waiting to be found (Winnicott, 1989).

This is a clinical insight about the nature of psychological development itself. The infant's first task is to achieve something more basic: the sense that experience can be meaningful, that inner life and outer reality can correspond, that the world is worth engaging with at all. This requires what Winnicott called "illusion"—the temporary experience of creating what one finds, of finding what one creates.

Such illusion depends entirely on environmental responsiveness. Abram's (2012) analysis reveals how this works clinically: when the mother presents the breast at the moment the infant begins to need it, the infant experiences having created the very thing that satisfies hunger. This is a developmental achievement to be protected—the basis of all later creativity, spontaneity, and engagement with reality. Without this early illusion of omnipotence, the infant may achieve intellectual understanding of the world while remaining fundamentally unengaged with it.

The clinical implications become clear when we consider what happens when this early illusion fails. The infant who never experiences creating what is found may develop what Winnicott called a "false self"—a compliant adaptation to environmental demands that leaves the spontaneous self hidden and unengaged. Such patients may function effectively in the world while feeling fundamentally unreal, cut off from their own aliveness.

For these patients, the analyst's interpretations can feel like impositions rather than discoveries, environmental demands rather than collaborative explorations. The therapeutic task becomes creating conditions within which the patient might finally experience the illusion of creating what they find—not through regression to literal infancy, but through the provision of a relationship that can be used creatively rather than merely adapted to.

The Limits of Innovation: Critical Perspectives on Winnicott's Departure from Classical Analysis

While Winnicott's contributions have been widely celebrated, they have generated substantial controversy about whether his innovations represent legitimate psychoanalytic developments or constitute a departure from its essential nature.

Rachel Blass presents a systematic critique challenging whether Winnicott's techniques remain within the psychoanalytic framework or fundamentally transgress its boundaries (Blass, 2012). She identifies three critical concerns: First, the transformation of the analyst from neutral interpreter to active, maternal figure providing holding and surviving attacks challenges traditional analytic neutrality. Second, his emphasis on non-symbolic, pre-object relating—"being together" rather than interpreting unconscious material—represents a fundamental departure from established technique. Third, the blurring of boundaries between psychoanalysis and supportive psychotherapy undermines the specificity of psychoanalytic intervention.

Horacio Etchegoyen provides additional theoretical grounding for these concerns, emphasizing the necessity of maintaining the analytic contract through a delicate balance between firmness in setting and responsiveness in style (Etchegoyen, 1991). His systematic survey of technical developments from Freud through Klein provides historical context for assessing whether Winnicott's contributions represent legitimate evolution or a break with psychoanalytic tradition.

Both critics acknowledge that Winnicott's techniques address important clinical phenomena, particularly with severely disturbed patients unresponsive to classical interpretation. However, they argue that the modifications required by his approach may compromise the essential characteristics distinguishing psychoanalysis from other therapeutic modalities. The controversy reflects broader tensions within contemporary psychoanalysis about balancing therapeutic responsiveness with analytic rigor—whether expanding the range of treatable patients justifies potential costs to theoretical coherence and technical precision.

Conclusion

The infant hallucinates the breast before finding it; the patient brings a dream before knowing what it means. What Winnicott discovered was that this sequence matters profoundly—that something must be created before it can be found, and that interpretation becomes therapeutic only when it arrives as the patient's own discovery rather than the analyst's delivery. The classical tradition emphasized what the analyst knows and when to say it. Winnicott shifted the question entirely: not what does the interpretation contain, but does the patient experience it as coming from within or as an intrusion from without? An interpretation that is accurate but premature violates the very capacity for experience it claims to illuminate. The analyst who knows too much too soon becomes, paradoxically, useless—or worse, becomes a seduction, inviting compliance rather than growth. This is why Winnicott could suggest that a brilliant interpretation, perfectly timed by the analyst's standards, might be the most anti-therapeutic intervention of all.

This requires a particular kind of analytic presence—not the disappeared analyst of caricature, but someone capable of what we might call "devoted attention" without therapeutic ambition. The analyst must be present enough to receive the patient's communications while remaining sufficiently opaque that the patient cannot simply merge with them to escape the fundamental aloneness that development requires.

Consider what this means for interpretation itself. When Winnicott notes that he interprets mainly to let the patient know the limits of his understanding, he points toward interpretation as a form of companionship with ignorance rather than a delivery of knowledge. The analyst's words become less important than their capacity to demonstrate that not-knowing can be sustained within relationship. This is interpretation as a form of play rather than instruction.

The temporal dimension becomes crucial here. Classical interpretation operates according to what might be called "revelatory time"—the analyst knows something the patient doesn't yet know and interpretation gradually closes this gap. Winnicott's approach follows "maturational time"—the patient's own developmental schedule, which cannot be accelerated through insight and may require periods where nothing interpretable occurs at all.

This creates space for what Winnicott called the "use of an object"—the patient's capacity to discover that their destructive impulses can be survived by someone who remains psychologically alive and available. This has nothing to do with the analyst becoming more loving or accepting; it requires them to be genuinely themselves in the encounter while not retaliating against the patient's inevitable attacks on their separateness.

The body emerges as central because he recognized that psychological development begins with the gradual integration of psyche and soma—a process that interpretation can disrupt if mistimed. The anorexic patient's belly pains were not symbols requiring decoding but actual somatic experiences seeking a relational context within which integration might eventually become possible.

This transforms our understanding of what psychoanalytic expertise involves. Rather than interpretive virtuosity, it requires what we might call "environmental attunement"—the capacity to provide the kinds of relational conditions within which the patient's own developmental processes can resume. This is more demanding, not less, than classical technique because it requires the analyst to function as both a separate person and as part of the patient's developmental matrix simultaneously.

The controversial dimension emerges precisely here: Winnicott's approach challenges the phantasy that psychoanalytic training can provide analysts with knowledge that patients lack. Instead, it suggests that analysis works through the provision of a particular kind of relationship within which patients can discover what they already know but have been unable to experience.

This does not eliminate the analyst's expertise but relocates it. The skill lies in the capacity to recognize and respond to different developmental needs as they emerge in the transference. Sometimes this means interpretation, sometimes holding, sometimes surviving the patient's use of the analyst as a transitional object.

What becomes possible is a different relationship to therapeutic failure. When classical interpretation fails, it suggests either incorrect understanding or patient resistance. When Winnicott's environmental approach fails, it often indicates that the analyst has moved too quickly, interpreted too early, or failed to provide adequate holding for the patient's developmental process.

Perhaps the most unsettling implication of Winnicott's work is how it reframes the question of therapeutic action entirely. Rather than asking "how do we help people to change?" it asks "how do we create conditions within which people can afford to be themselves?" This shift moves psychoanalysis away from its medical aspirations toward its deeper existentialist and humanistic roots—

toward the fundamental question of what it means to be, and to go on being.

This creates a curious paradox: the more successful Winnicott's approach becomes, the more it renders traditional psychoanalytic concepts obsolete. Terms like "resistance," "defense," and "working through" lose their explanatory power when the therapeutic action occurs through environmental provision rather than interpretive revelation. We are left with a psychoanalysis that no longer quite believes in its own classical vocabulary.

What emerges instead is something more provisional and experimental—a therapeutic practice that must invent itself anew with each patient because the analyst cannot know in advance what any particular person will need in order to begin living. This demands a kind of clinical improvisation and a willingness to be surprised by what becomes therapeutic in any given encounter.

The controversy Winnicott generated was not merely technical but existential: he forced psychoanalysis to confront its own exclusions, its own passion for ignorance about what human beings actually require in order to thrive. In refusing the comfort of interpretive certainty, he pointed toward something more difficult and more promising—the possibility that therapeutic work might be a form of collaborative wondering about what it means to be human.

References

Abram, J. (2012). On Winnicott's clinical innovations in the analysis of adults. *International Journal of Psychoanalysis*, 93(6), 1461–1473.

Blass, R. (2012). On Winnicott's clinical innovations in the analysis of adults: Introduction to a controversy. *International Journal of Psychoanalysis*, 93(6), 1439–1448.

Bollas, C. (2013). *Catch them before they fall: The psychoanalysis of breakdown*. Routledge.

Bonaminio, V. (2012). On Winnicott's clinical innovations in the analysis of adults. *International Journal of Psychoanalysis*, 93, 1475–1485.

Etchegoyen, R. H. (1991). *The fundamentals of psychoanalytic technique*. Karnac Books.

Freud, S. (1917). Introductory lectures on psycho-analysis. In J. Strachey (Ed. & Trans.), *The standard edition of the complete psychological works of Sigmund Freud* (Vol. 16). Hogarth Press.

Phillips, A. (1988). *Winnicott*. Fontana Press.

Segal, H. (1962). The curative factors in psychoanalysis. *International Journal of Psychoanalysis*, 43, 212–217.

Winnicott, D. W. (1954). Mind and its relation to the psyche-soma. *The British Journal of Medical Psychology*, 27(4), 201–209. doi:10.1111/j.2044-8341.1954.tb00864.x.

Winnicott, D. W. (1955). Metapsychological and clinical aspects of regression within the psychoanalytical set-up. *International Journal of Psychoanalysis*, 36, 16–26.

Winnicott, D. W. (1960). The theory of the parent-infant relationship. *International Journal of Psychoanalysis*, 41, 585–595.

Winnicott, D. W. (1963). The development of the capacity for concern. In *The maturational processes and the facilitating environment: Studies in the theory of emotional development* (pp. 73–82). Hogarth Press/Institute of Psychoanalysis.

Winnicott, D. W. (1965a). Child analysis in the latency period (1958). In *The maturational processes and the facilitating environment: Studies in the theory of emotional development* (pp. 115–123). Hogarth Press.

Winnicott, D. W. (1965b). The aims of psychoanalytical treatment (1962). In *The maturational processes and the facilitating environment: Studies in the theory of emotional development* (pp. 166–170). Hogarth Press.

Winnicott, D. W. (1965c). Classification: Is there a psycho-analytic contribution to psychiatric classification? (Original work written 1959–1964). In *The maturational processes and the facilitating environment: Studies in the theory of emotional development* (pp. 124–139). Hogarth Press.

Winnicott, D. W. (1966). Psycho-somatic illness in its positive and negative aspects. *International Journal of Psychoanalysis*, 47, 510–516.

Winnicott, D. W. (1969). The use of an object and relating through identifications. *International Journal of Psychoanalysis*, 50, 711–716.

Winnicott, D. W. (1971a). *Playing and reality*. Tavistock Publications.

Winnicott, D. W. (1971b). Case I: "Iiro" at 9 years 9 months. *Therapeutic Consultations in Child Psychiatry*, 87, 12–27.

Winnicott, D. W. (1986). *Holding and interpretation: Fragment of an analysis*. Hogarth Press.

Winnicott, D. W. (1989). The essential paradox for the individual. In C. Winnicott, R. Shepherd, & M. Davis (Eds.), *Psychoanalytic explorations* (p. 205). Harvard University Press.

Suggested Reading

Abram, J. (Ed.). (2013). *Donald Winnicott today*. Routledge.

Chapter 5

Interpretation in Heinz Kohut's Self Psychology

The Revolutionary Nature of Self Psychology's Approach to Interpretation

It is difficult today to fully grasp just how revolutionary Kohut's theoretical framework was for its time. The concept of empathy became the one of the first notions in psychoanalysis to genuinely rupture the conservative edifice that had long equated therapeutic action with interpretation leading to insight. This was no minor adjustment but a fundamental reconceptualization of the analytic enterprise itself.

Kohut emerged as the visionary whose ideas catalyzed a seismic shift from the established structural model of mental life to an understanding of the self as an integrated, dynamic whole. This reconceptualization unleashed a cascade of transformative insights: empathy was recognized as the fundamental medium of psychological existence. The self could only be understood as functioning within its matrix of selfobjects—we exist as complete beings solely through our connection with others, embodying a profound intersubjective reality. Human development itself was reimagined as unfolding within this essential context of otherness.

It is crucial to understand that in the United States of the 1970s and 1980s, Donald Winnicott's work remained largely unknown outside specialized circles. In this intellectual landscape, Heinz Kohut emerged as the most faithful representative of what I have termed in the previous chapter the "trauma healing" tradition in American psychoanalysis—that therapeutic lineage which prioritizes the restoration of developmental arrests and the

DOI: 10.4324/9781003590750-6

repair of early environmental failures over the archaeological excavation of repressed truth.

The historical moment demanded such a revolution. The scientific core of the psychoanalytic tradition had gradually calcified into rigid orthodoxy. The field had become paradoxically committed to ideals of individual autonomy while patients yearned for authentic connection; it remained fixated on austere notions of insight-through-interpretation while the post-war world cried out for genuine empathic understanding; it persisted in elaborate theories of guilt and neurosis even as the culture had evolved to embrace more nuanced, tragic dimensions of human experience.

Clinical practice, which had already begun to evolve beyond Freud's original prescriptions through the intuitive wisdom of practicing analysts, finally found in Kohut a theoretical architecture that could articulate why the most effective therapeutic approaches were those characterized by mutuality, openness, flexibility, and, above all, the analyst's profound empathic immersion in the patient's subjective world. What had been discovered intuitively in countless consulting rooms now possessed a coherent theoretical foundation.

However, Kohut's revolution was fundamentally clinical, not epistemological. While he transformed therapeutic practice by insisting that the analyst's subjectivity was essential to understanding and treating patients, he remained theoretically conservative, clinging to the scientific aspirations and truth-seeking ambitions of classical psychoanalysis. His concept of empathy as "vicarious introspection" attempted to preserve the objective, observational stance of traditional analysis even as his clinical work demonstrated that such objectivity was neither possible nor desirable. This tension between radical practice and conservative theory runs throughout his work—he brought the analyst's subjectivity through the front door clinically while trying to usher it out the back door theoretically.

Kohut's Early Formulations: The Paradox of Empathic Science

Kohut's paper "Introspection, Empathy, and Psychoanalysis" (1959) marked what would become a lifelong attempt to reconcile two fundamentally incompatible visions of psychological understanding. On the one hand, Kohut argued that was the only legitimate method for studying psychological phenomena. On the other hand, he insisted that this method was thoroughly scientific and capable of yielding objective truths about human experience in precisely the same way that other scientific instruments yield objective data about the physical world.

The tension here is revealing: Kohut's theoretical innovation—recognizing empathy as the fundamental mode of psychological observation—remained constrained by his insistence that this mode could yield scientific objectivity. Kohut seemed to sense this difficulty, which may explain why his relationship with traditional psychoanalytic authority was so ambivalent. Unlike later postmodern analysts who would explicitly reject the scientific pretensions of psychoanalysis, Kohut never abandoned his commitment to what he called "scientific objectivity." Even in his final writings, when he acknowledged that "objective truths must always include an assessment of the observer" (Kohut, 1984, p. 40), he continued to frame this insight as an advance in scientific understanding rather than a fundamental challenge to the scientific model itself.

This theoretical ambivalence must be understood partly in the context of Kohut's institutional position within American psychoanalysis. Unlike contemporary relational analysts who work largely outside traditional psychoanalytic institutions, Kohut was deeply embedded in the psychoanalytic establishment. He was a training analyst at the Chicago Institute, a former president of the American Psychoanalytic Association, and someone who clearly valued his position within mainstream psychoanalytic culture.

This institutional embeddedness may help to explain why Kohut was so careful to present his innovations as extensions rather than rejections of classical theory. In a 1978 letter Kohut wrote: "I am very eager not to encourage a break in the development of psychoanalysis and am therefore proceeding with theory change in a gradual way" (cited in Cocks, 1994). Even as late as 1978, three years before his death, Kohut was insisting that he was working "within psychoanalysis, not outside of it" (Cocks, 1994).

From Data-Gathering Tool to Therapeutic Experience

Perhaps nowhere is Kohut's evolving understanding more evident than in his changing conception of interpretation itself. In his early work, Kohut presented empathy primarily as a data-gathering tool—a more sophisticated way of collecting information about the patient's inner world that would then be processed through traditional interpretive frameworks. The analyst's empathic understanding was valuable, but it remained subordinate to the larger goal of providing accurate explanations of the patient's psychological functioning.

This recognition led Kohut to develop his famous distinction between "understanding" and "explaining" phases of interpretation (Kohut, 1984, p. 96). The understanding phase, he argued, involved the analyst's empathic immersion in the patient's subjective experience. Only after this foundation of empathic connection had been established could the explaining phase—offering genetic and dynamic interpretations—be therapeutically effective.

Yet even this more sophisticated model reveals Kohut's continued attachment to traditional therapeutic goals. The understanding phase, however valuable, remained in service of the explaining phase, which was where "real" therapeutic change supposedly occurred. As Kohut put it, the analyst's empathic understanding enables the patient to "become more objective vis-à-vis himself and his problems" (Kohut, 1984, p. 185). The ultimate goal remained essentially classical: helping the patient to achieve a more objective, reality-based perspective on their psychological functioning.

The Understanding Phase in Clinical Practice

The understanding phase of interpretation represents perhaps Kohut's most significant departure from classical technique. Here, the analyst's primary task is not to challenge defenses or to expose unconscious wishes but to enter empathically into the patient's subjective world. This requires what Kohut (1984) describes as "empathic immersion" in the patient's experience—a process of vicarious introspection that allows the analyst to grasp the patient's inner reality from within rather than observing it from without.

Clinical vignettes from Ernest Wolf illustrate the profound impact of this empathic understanding. In one case, Wolf (1993) describes a patient who spoke of being so eager to attend his session that he had driven through red traffic lights. Rather than interpreting this behavior in terms of transference love or aggressive acting out, Kohut's quick response—"you're a damn fool!"—was effective precisely because it communicated the analyst's genuine concern for the patient's well-being.

The understanding phase reveals itself as more paradoxical than Kohut's formulation initially suggests. When Kohut's patient drove through red traffic lights to reach his session, the analyst's response—calling him "a damn fool"—succeeded precisely because it failed to be traditionally interpretive. This moment exposes a curious reversal: the understanding phase works not by understanding in any conventional sense, but by providing something that resists understanding altogether—a spontaneous eruption of genuine concern that breaks through the interpretive machinery. The patient recognizes his excessive need to please not through the analyst's empathic grasp of this need, but through experiencing himself as someone who matters enough to provoke genuine alarm.

This suggests that what Kohut calls "empathic immersion" might be better understood as a kind of productive misunderstanding—a willingness to be surprised by the patient rather than to comprehend them. The analyst who truly enters the patient's subjective world must paradoxically abandon the very instruments of understanding that psychoanalysis has traditionally provided. When Kohut (1984) describes the analyst's task as grasping the patient's "perception of his psychic reality and accepts it as valid" (p. 173), he points toward something that exceeds the spatial metaphor he employs. In this sense, the analyst's "being within" the patient's world refers less to an inner location than to a stance in which theoretical mastery is set aside in favor of a willingness to be surprised and disoriented by the patient's experience.

The Explaining Phase as Retrospective Fiction

If the understanding phase operates through a kind of blessed incomprehension, the explaining phase—those genetic and dynamic interpretations that Kohut still considers essential—becomes something altogether more peculiar. Kohut insists that these explanations must follow the establishment of empathic connection, yet his clinical material suggests that explanation often serves to memorialize an understanding that has already done its work. The interpretation becomes not a tool for change but a monument to change that has already occurred—a way of making the ephemeral experience of being understood available for conscious reflection.

Consider Kohut's (1984, p. 116) analysis of the lawyer-patient whose intellectualization had protected him against his mother's invasive irrationality. Kohut came to recognize that what might traditionally be seen as "intellectualizing"—a defense-resistance impeding analysis—was actually a great achievement of the patient's early life. This "thinking machine" identity, as the patient conceived of himself, had successfully protected his self against his "a-little-crazy" mother's attempts to take him over. When Kohut explains this to the patient, the interpretation does not reveal hidden content but transforms the patient's relationship to something he had always known but never been able to fully recognize.

This distinction matters because it relocates the therapeutic action of interpretation. The explaining phase succeeds by offering what might be called a "witnessing vocabulary"—words that allow the patient's self-protective achievement to be recognized for what it truly is.

Optimal Frustration and Transmuting Internalization

Kohut's (1984) formulation that "psychoanalysis cures by the laying down of psychological structure" (p. 98) through optimal frustration and transmuting internalization offers a theory of therapeutic action that fundamentally reconceives the nature of psychic change. According to this view, the patient enters analysis with unmet developmental needs, seeking archaic forms of support from the analyst—mirroring that confirms their grandiosity, idealization that provides strength and calm, twinship that offers essential sameness. The analyst, through empathic attunement, temporarily fulfills these needs, yet inevitably cannot do so perfectly.

The mechanism Kohut proposes is transmuting internalization: through repeated cycles of empathic connection followed by tolerable disappointment, the patient gradually converts external selfobject functions into internal psychological structure. When the analyst's understanding falls short, the patient must momentarily provide their own self-soothing. When the idealized analyst proves human and fallible, the patient begins to access their own sources of strength. Each optimal frustration catalyzes a small act of self-provision that gradually accumulates into autonomous capacity.

A clinical vignette from Kohut's practice (1984, p. 182) illuminates the delicate nature of this process. Following an absence, Kohut's patient experienced a severe deterioration—painful head sensations, quasi-paranoid accusations about the harshness of people's voices, and even taking his television to a repair shop to check if it had been tampered with. Kohut initially offered what seemed like empathic interpretations: he suggested that the patient's worsening was paradoxically part of his improvement, that increased emotional openness had exposed him to new anxieties. While cognitively correct, these interpretations only temporarily relieved the patient's distress before he returned to attacking Kohut as lacking all understanding.

What Kohut gradually came to grasp was that his interpretations, however accurate, constituted an additional trauma. The patient experienced them as coming "only from the outside"—words without real understanding, thereby repeating the essential trauma of his early life. The crucial therapeutic shift occurred when Kohut (1984) stopped defending the correctness of his interpretations and instead allowed himself to see things "exclusively in his way and not at all in my way" (p. 182). This required Kohut to undergo his own painful process of self-scrutiny, examining the inner barriers that prevented him from fully feeling what the patient felt.

This represents a radical revision of analytic technique. The analyst must accept the patient's criticism not as transference distortion to be interpreted but as psychological truth to be embraced. Kohut had to undergo his own painful process of self-scrutiny, examining why his interpretations, however accurate, came "only from the outside"—why he gave words but not real understanding, thereby repeating the essential trauma of the patient's early life.

This clinical sequence reveals how optimal frustration operates at multiple levels simultaneously. The initial frustration—Kohut's absence—triggered archaic needs and primitive anxieties. But the more significant frustration emerged in the gap between Kohut's cognitive understanding and emotional attunement. The patient needed Kohut to experience his world from within, not explain it from without. Paradoxically, it was Kohut's acceptance of his own empathic failure, his willingness to persist despite the patient's attacks and his own defensive reactions, that eventually allowed genuine contact to emerge.

The transmuting internalization occurred through the patient discovering, within the crucible of misunderstanding and gradual repair, his own capacity to maintain self-cohesion even when profoundly misrecognized.

This suggests that optimal frustration involves something more complex than the analyst's minor, inevitable failures. It encompasses the entire dimension of otherness that analysis must navigate—the fact that even the most devoted analyst remains fundamentally separate, seeing through their own eyes, shaped by their own history. The patient builds structure not by internalizing what the analyst provides but by developing ways to bridge this irreducible gap. When Kohut (1984) notes that understanding "substitutes for the de facto fulfillment of the patient's need" (p. 102), he points toward this paradox: the need for perfect mirroring gives way to the capacity to sustain oneself despite imperfect recognition.

The Paradox of Structure Building

The process by which optimal frustrations become psychic structure remains, in Kohut's account, fundamentally mysterious. He speaks of "transmuting internalization," but this term names rather than explains the alchemy by which relational experiences become autonomous capacities. How does the repeated experience of being understood become the ability to understand oneself? How does the analyst's recognition of mistakes become the patient's capacity for self-reflection?

Kohut's clinical material suggests that structure building might be less about internalization than about discovering capacities that were always present but couldn't be accessed without the safety of the analytic relationship. The lawyer-patient's ability to laugh, to express emotion, to relax—these weren't newly created capacities but recovered possibilities that had been sacrificed in the service of psychological survival.

This reconceptualization has profound implications for how we understand therapeutic change. The analyst doesn't give the patient something new but creates conditions in which the patient can reclaim what was always theirs. The selfobject functions that the analyst provides don't become internalized; rather, they make it possible for the patient to recognize and utilize selfobject experiences that were always available but couldn't be trusted.

The Analyst as Selfobject

Kohut's recognition that the analyst functions as a selfobject rather than merely an interpreter of unconscious content revolutionizes our understanding of therapeutic action. In his final work, he delineates three principal selfobject transferences—mirroring, idealizing, and twinship, which represent "the self's active attempt at healing and finishing its interrupted development" (Kohut, 1984, p. 103). The patient who seeks the analyst's admiring gaze, who needs to idealize the analyst's strength, or who requires the analyst to be fundamentally alike, enacts developmental strivings that were thwarted in early life.

This reconceptualization transforms interpretation itself into a selfobject function. When the analyst offers an interpretation, they provide what Kohut calls a responsive selfobject experience. The therapeutic power lies less in the interpretation's accuracy than in its demonstration that the patient exists in the analyst's mind as someone worth sustained, careful thought. Each interpretive effort, whether correct or mistaken, performs a mirroring function—confirming that the patient's inner life merits deep engagement and persistent effort to understand.

This is why Kohut insists that "the analyst's primary tool must be sustained, finely attuned empathy—not interpretation as revelation of hidden drive conflicts" (Kohut, 1984, p. 115). The distinction matters profoundly. In Kohut's framework, interpretation works through providing the missing developmental experience—the experience of being accurately perceived, deeply considered, patiently held in another's attention even when one is attacking, withdrawing, or falling apart.

When the analyst struggles to understand, revises their understanding, acknowledges their failure and tries again, they demonstrate something more valuable than perfect empathy: they show that the patient is worth the ongoing effort of understanding, worth returning to after failure, worth thinking about even when they are at their most difficult or attacking.

Yet this formulation raises uncomfortable questions about the nature of psychoanalytic cure. If the analyst functions primarily as a selfobject, providing through their reliable attention what was missing in early development, how does this differ from what Kohut calls the patient's need for selfobjects throughout life? The cure, then, is not independence from selfobjects but what he describes as "the patient's newfound ability to seek, recognize, and draw on selfobjects outside therapy" (Kohut, 1984, p. 120).

This suggests that analysis teaches something quite specific: how to recognize and use available selfobject experiences rather than either desperately seeking perfect mirroring or defensively denying all need for others. The patient who can only accept perfect understanding learns, through the analyst's failures and repairs, to make use of imperfect but good-enough responsiveness. The patient who cannot bear to need anyone discovers, through the reliability of the analytic relationship, that dependence need not lead to traumatic disappointment.

The most radical implication of Kohut's theory (1984) may be its suggestion that psychological structure itself develops through relationship—that what we call the "self" is not an autonomous entity but a dynamic organization that exists only within what he terms the "matrix of selfobjects." The analyst as selfobject does not provide something to the patient, but rather creates the conditions within which the patient's self can cohere, vitalize, and develop. The interpretation that works is the one that performs this self-object function, regardless of its content—the one that allows the patient to experience themselves as real, valuable, and capable of growth within the responsive field of another's attention.

Beyond Interpretation

The ultimate implication of Kohut's clinical and theoretical revolution—one his epistemological conservatism prevented him from fully articulating—is that interpretation as traditionally conceived becomes something entirely different. If therapeutic action lies in the experience of being understood rather than in the content of understanding, if explanation works by witnessing rather than revealing, if resistance protects hope rather than hiding truth, then interpretation cannot be about uncovering objective psychological truths. Kohut's revolutionary concepts—selfobject transferences, transmuting internalization, optimal frustration—all point toward this conclusion, yet he continued to frame them within a traditional epistemological framework. What remains of interpretation when we recognize that it creates relational realities rather than discovers hidden truths?

Kohut's clinical work points toward a practice by which the analyst's task becomes to recognize the intelligence of the patient's solutions to impossible situations. This is not a matter of validation or affirmation but of seeing clearly what the patient has always known but couldn't know alone.

The profound transformation this represents becomes clear in Kohut's treatment of the lawyer-patient's relationship to his father. Classical analysis might interpret the patient's fear of his father's weakness as a defense against competitive or homosexual wishes. Kohut recognizes it as exactly what it appears to be—a child's accurate perception that his father couldn't provide the idealizable strength he needed. The interpretation doesn't reveal hidden content but confirms the patient's reality, a reality that had been systematically invalidated by those who should have confirmed it.

This movement from interpretation to recognition represents more than a technical modification. It acknowledges that patients often know exactly what's wrong; what they don't know is that they know it, or that their knowledge matters, or that anyone else can bear to know it with them. The analyst's function becomes not to provide new knowledge but to create conditions in which the patient's own knowledge can be recognized, valued, and utilized.

The implications extend beyond the consulting room. If human beings never transcend their need for selfobject experiences, if psychological health means effective dependency rather than autonomy, if our defenses protect hope rather than hide forbidden wishes, then psychoanalysis must fundamentally revise not just its technique but its understanding of human nature. Kohut opened this door but couldn't quite walk through it, perhaps sensing that what lay beyond would require abandoning too much of what had made psychoanalysis what it was.

Kohut's institutional embeddedness and theoretical commitments prevented him from fully embracing this insight's radical implications: that interpretation as traditionally conceived is obsolete, and what patients need is not explanation but recognition—having their adaptive intelligence witnessed and confirmed by another mind. This unfinished revolution points toward a fundamental reconceptualization of therapeutic action: from decoding the unconscious to recognizing the wisdom in what was always visible but systematically invalidated.

The Co-Creative Nature of Interpretation

Ernest Wolf's collaboration with Joseph Lichtenberg in their 1997 position statement on self psychology reveals how far the field had evolved since Kohut's death. They write: "Self psychology takes the stand that the baby is innately 'strong.' We are born preadapted to respond to an empathically sensitive family life that reliably provides soothing, vitalizing, and need-fulfilling experiences" (Lichtenberg & Wolf, 1997, p. 536). This optimistic view of human nature represents a significant departure from classical psychoanalytic pessimism about human destructiveness.

But perhaps more importantly, Lichtenberg and Wolf articulate a vision of therapeutic action that is fundamentally intersubjective: "During an ongoing treatment both patient and therapist communicate verbally and nonverbally, thereby providing a basis for selfobject experiences for the other" (Lichtenberg & Wolf, 1997, p. 533). This mutual influence means that interpretation can never be a one-way delivery of truth from analyst to patient. It's always a collaborative creation, shaped by both participants' contributions.

The epistemological shift here is radical. Where Kohut had maintained that empathy provided a relatively objective mode of observation—"vicarious introspection"—Wolf and Lichtenberg acknowledge that even empathic perception is shaped by the observer's subjectivity. They note that "information derived from other sources such as studies of infant development, forms of memory, subliminal perception, affect communication, nonreflective cognition, and neurophysiology enriches our understanding of information derived from an empathic mode of perception" (Lichtenberg & Wolf, 1997, p. 532). This integration of multiple perspectives represents a more epistemologically humble stance than Kohut's—an acknowledgment that no single mode of observation, however empathic, can capture the full complexity of human experience.

Conclusion: The Unfinished Revolution

Where does this leave us? Kohut's legacy is a sophisticated paradox: it is an ethic of presence without possessiveness, of knowing without mastery, of intervening without coercion. If analysis cures, it cures not through the analyst's superior knowledge, but through an encounter that allows the patient to borrow, for a time, the analyst's faith that a story—any story—is worth the effort to tell. This borrowed faith becomes something more profound than cure in any traditional sense—it becomes the patient's discovery that their particular way of surviving was never pathology but meaning, never symptom but solution.

The tragedy and triumph of Kohut's contribution is that he gave us the tools to dismantle the very edifice he sought to preserve. As I wrote elsewhere (Govrin, 2025), "as he refuses to relinquish the truth of interpretation and in his efforts to base this truth on subjective element, Kohut exposes himself to irresolvable contradictions" (p. 81). His careful observations of therapeutic action revealed that what actually works in analysis cannot be grounded in the kind of interpretive truth Kohut tried to secure and instead exposes the very contradictions he could not resolve.

Kohut's work opens the way toward a different vision of analysis—one he could not fully claim— in which the consulting room is not where we transcend our need for others but where we learn to need them well. The analyst's ultimate gift is not insight but companionship in the difficult work of recognizing what we have always known: that our strangest adaptations were our sanest responses, that our resistances protected our hopes, and that what we call pathology might simply be the cost of staying alive in situations that offered no better options. In this light, the question is not whether psychoanalysis can survive the loss of interpretation as its central organizing principle, but whether it can flourish by embracing what has always been its secret strength—the radical act of taking another person seriously enough to believe that their suffering makes sense.

References

Cocks, G. (Ed.). (1994). *The curve of life: Correspondence of Heinz Kohut, 1923–1981*. University of Chicago Press.

Feiner, K., & Kiersky, S. (1994). Empathy is perception and interpretation (and who ever said it wasn't?): Reply to Ghent and Stern. *Psychoanalytic Dialogues*, 4(3), 487–497.

Ghent, E. (1994). Empathy—whence and whither?: Commentary on papers by Kiersky and Beebe, Hayes, and Feiner and Kiersky. *Psychoanalytic Dialogues*, 4(3), 473–486.

Govrin, A. (2025). *How philosophy changed psychoanalysis: From naïve realism to postmodernism*. Routledge.
Kernberg, O. F. (2000). A concerned critique of psychoanalytic education. *International Journal of Psychoanalysis*, 81, 97–120.
Kohut, H. (1959). Introspection, empathy, and psychoanalysis: An examination of the relationship between mode of observation and theory. *Journal of the American Psychoanalytic Association*, 7, 459–483.
Kohut, H. (1984). *How Does Analysis Cure?* (A. Goldberg, Ed.). University of Chicago Press.
Lichtenberg, J., & Wolf, E. (1997). General principles of self psychology: A position statement. *Journal of the American Psychoanalytic Association*, 45, 531–543.
Ornstein, A. (1991). The dread to repeat: Comments on the working-through process in psychoanalysis. *Journal of the American Psychoanalytic Association*, 39, 377–398.
Stern, D. B. (1994). Empathy is interpretation (and who ever said it wasn't?): Commentary on papers by Hayes, Kiersky and Beebe, and Feiner and Kiersky. *Psychoanalytic Dialogues*, 4(3), 441–471.
Wolf, E. (1992). The role of interpretation in therapeutic change. *Progress in Self Psychology*, 9, 15–30.
Wolf, E. (1993). Disruptions of the therapeutic relationship in psychoanalysis: A view from self psychology. *International Journal of Psycho-Analysis*, 74, 675–687.

Suggested Reading

Kohut, H. (1984). *How does analysis cure?* (A. Goldberg, Ed.). University of Chicago Press.

Chapter 6

Interpretation in Relational Psychoanalysis

For decades, psychoanalysts occupied a kind of interpretive Olympus, gazing down at their patients with the confidence of those who possessed the key to the unconscious. The analyst was the one who knew; the patient was the one who needed to know. Interpretation flowed in one direction, from the analyst's superior vantage point into the patient's confused interior. This model, elegant in its simplicity, rested on a fundamental assumption: that the analyst could achieve sufficient objectivity to render accurate judgments about another person's psychic reality.

But upon closer inspection the analyst's interpretation reveals itself to be radically different from how it first appears. What presents itself as an unveiling of the patient's unconscious truth turns out to be something altogether more curious: a disclosure of the analyst's own psychic configuration, dressed in the costume of clinical insight. We might say that every interpretation is a kind of accidental self-portrait, painted while the artist believes he is capturing someone else's likeness.

The relational turn in psychoanalysis has made explicit what was always implicit: that the consulting room contains not one unconscious but two, not one set of conflicts but a proliferation of them, not one truth waiting to be discovered but a proliferation of truths waiting to be invented. The analyst's authority, so carefully cultivated and so anxiously preserved, dissolves into something more interesting—a collaborative uncertainty in which both parties find themselves equally implicated.

What emerges is not the collapse of psychoanalytic knowledge, but its liberation from the fantasy of objectivity. In this space

DOI: 10.4324/9781003590750-7

between two subjectivities, something genuinely new becomes possible: not the revelation of what was always already there, but the creation of what has never before existed.

The psychoanalytic interpretation has always been a curious instrument—simultaneously an act of revelation and concealment, a gesture toward truth that invariably discloses the interpreter's own psychic geography. Yet it is only with the relational turn in psychoanalysis that this paradox has been fully embraced rather than defensively managed.

The transformation of the relational approach rests on a deceptively simple recognition articulated by Lewis Aron (1992): "interpretation is best thought of as the quintessential container and purveyor of intersubjectivity between patient and analyst" (p. 475). This single formulation dismantles the edifice of analytic authority that had sustained psychoanalysis for nearly a century. If interpretation is inherently intersubjective, then the analyst's unconscious, theoretical preferences, personal history, and emotional responses inevitably shape not only what they hear but what becomes speakable in the analytic space. As Aron (1992) observes with characteristic precision:

> The analyst is not only impacted by his own unconscious process in the formulation of any interpretation, not only a full participant in any analytic enactment, but partially blind to the role he plays in helping the patient to understand both of these processes.
>
> (p. 654)

What emerges is a model of therapeutic action that depends not on the transmission of preexisting truths but on the generation of new meanings that neither participant could have discovered by themselves.

If interpretation no longer functions as the revelation of hidden truths but instead raises troubling questions, what exactly does it accomplish? The relational answer, as we shall see, involves a radical reconceptualization of both the nature of unconscious communication and the mechanisms of psychic change.

Through examining four interrelated dimensions of this reconceptualization—enactment as the medium of unconscious communication, dissociation as the structure of psychic organization, the analytic third, and self-disclosure as the vehicle of authentic engagement—we can begin to understand how the relational approach transforms interpretation from an epistemological exercise into an ontological encounter.

Enactment: The Unconscious in Action

The concept of enactment has become central to relational psychoanalysis precisely because it captures something that traditional interpretation could never quite grasp: the way unconscious communication occurs not through symbolic representation but through lived experience. Anthony Bass (2003) makes a crucial distinction between ordinary enactments—the quotidian mutual influences that texture every analytic hour—and what he terms capital-E Enactments, those moments when "unconscious psychic elements in patient and analyst mobilize our full, heightened attention and define, and take hold of, analytic activity for periods of time" (p. 657). These Enactments, Bass suggests, often emerge through "mistakes, slips, and blind spots that serve as doors through which the analyst and the patient are transported into realms of personal encounter and self-experience that might otherwise remain inaccessible" (660).

Rather than standing outside the patient's dynamics to interpret them, the analyst is inevitably drawn into enacting complementary roles. The therapeutic action emerges not from the analyst's capacity to understand and explain these enactments but from both participants' ability to survive and metabolize them together. The most profound therapeutic moments often occur precisely when both participants' defensive organizations temporarily collapse, creating space for something genuinely new to emerge.

Stephen Mitchell's (2000) clinical work with Ed provides a compelling illustration of how enactments serve as both revelation and creation of meaning.

The enactment that Mitchell describes began with his forgetting an early morning appointment he had scheduled to accommodate Ed's dental emergency. Finding Ed waiting in the bitter cold, Mitchell apologized and hurried them inside. Ed's response—"So, you're a creature of habit"—initiated a complex dance around guilt, reparation, and the possibility of ordinary human fallibility. When Mitchell charged Ed one-third of the usual fee for their abbreviated session, Ed was furious, experiencing this as petty and ungenerous. Mitchell's decision not to waive the fee emerged from his recognition that doing so would constitute "appeasing him, buying him off"—perpetuating rather than transforming Ed's internal world where guilt must always be erased through reparative action rather than borne as part of human experience.

What makes this vignette particularly instructive is how it demonstrates that interpretation in the relational model emerges through rather than about enactment. Mitchell doesn't simply interpret Ed's reaction; he participates in creating a new relational experience where guilt can be tolerated rather than evacuated, where imperfection doesn't require compensation, where two people can fail each other and remain in a relationship.

The confidence with which Mitchell later explains his motivations may itself be defensive, turning a moment of genuine uncertainty into a theoretical explanation.

These ambiguities are not failures of the relational approach, but rather its most honest acknowledgment: that every interpretation, even those emerging through enactment, remains irreducibly ambiguous, open to multiple meanings that can never be fully resolved.

The therapeutic action emerges not from the analyst's capacity to stand outside and interpret these enactments but from both participants' ability to survive and metabolize them together. As Mitchell (1988) noted, unless the analyst affectively enters the patient's relational matrix and discovers themselves within it—becoming charmed by the patient's entreaties, shaped by the patient's projections, and antagonized and frustrated by the patient's defenses—the treatment never fully engages and a certain depth is lost. This formulation challenges traditional notions of analytic neutrality and positions the analyst as an inevitable participant whose very participation becomes the vehicle for therapeutic change. The interpretation doesn't explain the enactment; rather, the lived experience of navigating the enactment together, with all its uncertainties and ambiguities, constitutes the interpretive work itself.

Dissociation, Enactment, and the Transformation of Interpretation: Philip Bromberg's Revolutionary Vision

The Dissociative Gap as Clinical Reality

Philip Bromberg's (2010) central insight concerns what he terms "minding the dissociative gap", that is, the recognition that therapeutic action emerges through the shared navigation of dissociated experience rather than through traditional interpretive unveiling. The mind, in Bromberg's vision, operates as a collection of self-states that may exist in protective isolation from one another, particularly when trauma has rigidified the normal flow between different aspects of experience.

The analyst's task becomes radically different when viewed through this lens. Rather than interpreting unconscious conflicts, the analyst must recognize and work with the patient's multiple self-states, understanding that what appears as resistance often represents the protective dissociation of "not-me" aspects of experience.

Bromberg's understanding of enactment moves beyond traditional notions of acting out or projective identification. Enactments represent moments when both analyst and patient become locked into dissociative processes, each defending against "not-me" aspects of experience by unconsciously inducing these aspects in the other.

The interpretive challenge becomes recognizing these mutual dissociative processes as they unfold. Traditional interpretation might address the patient's defensive perfectionism or the analyst's countertransference reactions as separate phenomena. Bromberg's approach recognizes the enactment as a co-created dissociative field where both participants are simultaneously enacting and disowning aspects of shared emotional reality.

Metaphor, Cooccurrence, and Symbolic Transformation

Stern's (2009) exploration of metaphor and cooccurrence extends Bromberg's thinking into the realm of symbolic process. The therapeutic task involves creating conditions where cooccurrences can be recognized and developed into metaphorical understanding. This process cannot be forced through interpretation; it emerges through the gradual softening of dissociative barriers as different self-states become more comfortable with each other's existence. The analyst's capacity to tolerate and work with their own dissociative reactions becomes crucial, as it models the possibility of holding contradictory aspects of experience simultaneously.

Bromberg's approach demands a fundamental reconsideration of interpretive technique. The analyst must listen for self-state shifts rather than unconscious content, attending to sudden changes in topic, affects, or ways of being that signal movement between different organizations of experience (Bromberg, 2010). The goal becomes facilitating communication between self-states rather than making unconscious material conscious.

Bromberg illustrates this with his description of working with patients who use "conflict language" (2010, p. 23) while actually being dissociated. A patient might say they are trying hard to feel confident instead of afraid but cannot seem to get it right. Bromberg recognizes that the phrase "instead of" represents false conflict language—the patient is not actually experiencing internal conflict but is attempting to obliterate one self-state to please the analyst. His intervention addresses this directly: he might observe that there seems to be another part of them behind the scenes that does not like what he just said, and that they appear to be trying to keep their relationship safe by staying away from those unruly feelings. Rather than interpreting the fear as resistance to confidence, he recognizes two legitimate self-states that need to coexist rather than one eliminating the other.

This shift requires what Bromberg calls a different "listening stance" (1910. p. 20)—one that attends to the inherently confusing nature of clinical process rather than seeking to organize it into coherent understanding. The analyst must tolerate not knowing while remaining present to the patient's struggle to integrate disparate aspects of experience. Interpretation, when it occurs, emerges from this shared process of discovery rather than from the analyst's theoretical understanding.

The clinical material Stern (2009) presents demonstrates this approach in action. He describes working with an attractive, accomplished woman who sought treatment because, despite her apparent perfection, she could not maintain lasting romantic relationships. For months, Stern found himself feeling inadequate and incompetent, unable to penetrate what he experienced as her flawless presentation. The patient maintained a brittle cheerfulness that seemed to deflect any genuine contact, while Stern struggled with the sense that his interpretations were vapid and unhelpful. Both were locked in a mutual enactment—she presenting an impossible perfection while he absorbed the shame of professional inadequacy. The breakthrough came not through a brilliant interpretation but through Stern's authentic recognition of the patient's underlying loneliness—a recognition that emerged from his willingness to tolerate his own shame and inadequacy long enough for a new perception to form. When he finally spoke about her vulnerability and isolation, she wept and acknowledged that she had indeed always been lonely and had never felt truly known by anyone. The interpretation was co-created through the relational process rather than delivered from outside it.

Shame, Recognition, and Therapeutic Action

Bromberg's emphasis on shame as a central organizing force in dissociative processes has profound implications for interpretive work. Shame often represents the affective signal that certain aspects of experience must remain "not-me" to preserve attachment bonds. The therapeutic relationship becomes a laboratory for experimenting with new forms of recognition that do not provoke the shame-dissociation cycle.

The analyst's interpretive task involves recognizing the patient's dissociated self-states without inadvertently inducing shame through premature integration attempts. This requires extraordinary sensitivity to the patient's capacity to tolerate self-reflection at any given moment. The interpretation must emerge from a place of genuine recognition rather than theoretical understanding, as only such recognition can provide the safety necessary for integration to occur.

Critical Reflections on the Dissociative Turn

Yet Bromberg's emphasis on mutual enactment and shared dissociation raises intriguing questions about the nature of analytic understanding itself. The risk inherent in Bromberg's approach may be the gradual erosion of what makes psychoanalysis distinctively analytic. When the analyst becomes so focused on managing dissociative enactments and facilitating self-state communication, the capacity for sustained thought about unconscious process may atrophy. The analyst's mind, constantly alert to relational nuance and affective shifts, may lose the contemplative quality that allows for deeper pattern recognition across time. While Bromberg would argue that this represents an evolution beyond outdated models of analytic neutrality, critics might suggest that it represents a fundamental departure from the reflective stance that enables genuine psychological insight. The question remains whether therapeutic effectiveness requires the analyst to sacrifice a certain kind of analytic rigor in favor of relational authenticity, and whether such sacrifice ultimately serves or undermines the therapeutic process.

The Analytic Third: Interpretation as Emergent Property

The concept of the analytic third represents perhaps the most radical departure from traditional psychoanalytic epistemology, fundamentally reconceptualizing where interpretation originates and how therapeutic meaning emerges. Neither residing in the patient's unconscious waiting to be discovered, nor in the analyst's mind waiting to be delivered, interpretation in this model emerges from what Thomas Ogden (2004) calls the analytic third—a jointly created unconscious space that exists between and beyond both participants. This third space transforms interpretation from an act of decoding into an emergent property of the analytic relationship itself.

Ogden's formulation of the analytic third posits that patient and analyst create something that transcends their individual psychologies—a shared unconscious space with its own characteristics, dynamics, and generative potential (Ogden, 1994, 1997). This third is not simply the sum of two subjectivities, but rather a dialectical creation that simultaneously preserves and negates the separateness of each participant. The analyst and patient remain distinct individuals while also becoming something else together—participants in a jointly created unconscious life that belongs fully to neither yet profoundly influences both.

If the most significant unconscious dynamics exist not within either participant but in the space between them, then interpretation cannot be a unidirectional delivery of insight. This interpretation emerges from within the third rather than being applied to it from outside.

Jessica Benjamin's concept of thirdness extends this understanding into the realm of recognition and intersubjective space (Benjamin, 2004, 2018). For Benjamin, the third represents the principle of mediation that makes genuine recognition possible—the space where both participants can simultaneously maintain their own subjectivity while recognizing the other's separate existence. This third space is fragile and constantly under threat of collapse into what Benjamin terms "doer and done to" dynamics, where complementarity replaces mutuality and recognition fails.

The relationship between thirdness and interpretation becomes particularly significant in Benjamin's model. When the third collapses—when the analytic pair falls into complementary dynamics where one person becomes subject and the other object—interpretation in any meaningful sense becomes impossible. What masquerades as interpretation in such moments is actually enactment, with one person imposing meaning on the other rather than both participating in the creation of shared understanding. The restoration of thirdness becomes a precondition for genuine interpretive work.

Benjamin's clinical illustrations demonstrate how the collapse and restoration of thirdness shapes interpretive possibility. When analyst and patient become locked in complementary patterns—the analyst as knower and patient as known, or patient as victim and analyst as rescuer—the third space disappears and with it the possibility of genuine interpretation. The work involves not interpreting these dynamics from outside but recognizing how both participants contribute to their creation and perpetuation. The interpretation emerges through the mutual recognition of how both have participated in the collapse of thirdness and their shared effort to restore it.

This temporal complexity manifests clinically in moments when an interpretation seems to create the very reality it purports to describe. An analyst might offer an understanding that neither participant could have articulated before, yet once spoken, it seems to have always been true. This is not because the interpretation revealed something hidden but because it emerged from and gave form to the inchoate experience of the third.

The clinical implications extend to the very structure of interpretive intervention. Rather than the analyst formulating an interpretation internally and then deciding whether and how to deliver it, interpretations in the model of the third emerge through a more collaborative process. The analyst might begin a thought that the patient completes, or the patient might offer an association that suddenly crystallizes something the analyst had been sensing but couldn't articulate. The interpretation belongs to neither and both simultaneously.

This collaborative emergence doesn't imply symmetry or equality—the analyst retains specific responsibilities and functions that differ from those of the patient. But it does mean that the analyst's interpretive authority derives not from superior knowledge or objectivity but from their capacity to attend to and articulate what emerges in the third. The analyst serves as what Ogden calls a "host" to the analytic third, maintaining conditions for its existence while remaining open to being transformed by what emerges within it.

The concept of the third also transforms our understanding of resistance to interpretation. When a patient rejects or seems unable to use an interpretation, this might indicate not resistance in the traditional sense but the absence of a viable third space where the interpretation could take root and grow. The therapeutic task becomes not overcoming resistance but creating conditions where thirdness can emerge and sustain itself long enough for interpretive work to occur.

The relationship between the third and trauma adds another dimension to interpretive complexity. Traumatic experience often destroys the capacity for thirdness, trapping individuals in rigid self-other configurations that preclude genuine intersubjective meeting. The interpretive task with traumatized patients involves not primarily explaining or understanding trauma but gradually rebuilding the capacity for thirdness—creating conditions where interpretation becomes possible rather than retraumatizing.

This understanding shifts the focus from the content of interpretations to their function in maintaining and developing the third. An interpretation might be valuable not because it accurately captures unconscious meaning but because it demonstrates the analyst's ongoing engagement with the shared creative process. The patient experiences not just being understood but participating in the creation of understanding—a fundamentally different therapeutic action from receiving insight from another.

The analytic third also illuminates the limitations and possibilities of interpretive work. If interpretation emerges from the third rather than being delivered to it, then the richness and depth of interpretive possibility depends on the vitality of the third itself. A constricted or fragile third will generate limited interpretive possibilities, while a robust third can produce interpretations of surprising depth and transformative power. The analyst's skill lies not primarily in formulating clever interpretations but in fostering conditions where the third can flourish.

Yet questions remain about the ontological status of the third. Is it a metaphor for describing complex relational dynamics, or does it refer to something that actually exists in some form? Different theorists take different positions on this question, but what matters clinically is that working as if the third exists—attending to it, nurturing it, interpreting from within it—produces different therapeutic effects than working from a two-person psychology that doesn't recognize this emergent dimension.

The concept of the third ultimately suggests that interpretation in relational psychoanalysis is neither a technical procedure nor a hermeneutic exercise but a creative act that brings new realities into being. The interpretation doesn't decode what exists but participates in creating what might become possible. This creative dimension doesn't diminish the rigor or discipline of interpretive work but locates these qualities in the service of generative possibility rather than archaeological discovery.

Self-Disclosure and the Question of Analytic Authority

The relational approach to analyst self-disclosure represents perhaps the most controversial aspect of this theoretical revolution. What was once forbidden territory has become, in relational hands, a sophisticated clinical instrument. Yet as Steven Kuchuck's (2009, 2021) careful exploration reveals, self-disclosure is never simply a technical decision but always an ethical encounter with the analyst's own narcissistic and self-regulatory needs.

Kuchuck's concept of "silent-disclosure" (2018)—those internal deliberations about sharing that may themselves be therapeutic even when they remain unspoken—captures something essential about the relational position. The analyst's subjectivity is always present, always influential, whether acknowledged or not. The question is not whether to be subjective but how to use one's subjectivity in the service of the patient's growth.

The case Kuchuck (2009) presents of his work with Sam, a gay man struggling with the decision about whether to have children, illustrates the complexity of these decisions. Kuchuck, facing his own unresolved feelings about childlessness, chooses not to disclose his similar situation despite Sam's apparent wish for connection through shared experience. This decision emerges from both clinical judgment and personal vulnerability—a recognition that disclosure at this moment would serve both his and Sam's defensive needs to avoid the painful singularity of their respective experiences.

This vignette reveals how self-disclosure decisions are always overdetermined, containing multiple motivations that can never be fully disentangled. The analyst may disclose out of loneliness, a wish to be seen, or to manage their own discomfort. Conversely, they may withhold disclosure to maintain an idealized image, avoid vulnerability, or manage guilt and shame. The relational position doesn't resolve these ambiguities but insists on acknowledging them as intrinsic to the analytic process.

Jay Greenberg's (2001) critique provides a necessary counterpoint to the enthusiasm surrounding analyst self-disclosure. His observation that relational case examples invariably portray analysts who "throw away the book" in moments of crisis raises important questions about whose needs are being served. In a profession under siege, analysts may be particularly vulnerable to what Greenberg calls "therapeutic zeal"—the wish to rescue, to heal, to transform through personal engagement rather than analytic understanding.

Greenberg's most provocative suggestion is that the relational emphasis on creating novel experiences may actually foreclose deeper engagement with the patient's psychic reality. When the analyst acts quickly to provide a corrective experience, they may prevent both participants from fully confronting the depth and intensity of the patient's transference. Jon Mills (2017) extends this critique, arguing that excessive emphasis on mutuality risks ignoring the fundamental asymmetries that structure the analytic relationship—primarily that the patient seeks help and that the analyst is being paid as an authority.

These critiques don't invalidate the relational approach, but rather highlight its inherent tensions. The question is not whether to be personal or impersonal, mutual or asymmetrical, but how to navigate these polarities in ways that serve the therapeutic process. The relational position, at its best, maintains creative tension between connection and reflection, engagement and analysis, mutuality and asymmetry.

Conclusion: The Relational Revolution at the Crossroads

The relational transformation of psychoanalytic interpretation represents one of the most significant developments in contemporary psychoanalysis, embodying both the promise and complexity of theoretical evolution. What began as a necessary corrective to the authoritarian certainties of classical psychoanalysis—where the analyst served as oracle, interpretation as archaeological truth, and the patient as passive recipient of insight—has matured into a nuanced approach that has fundamentally enriched our understanding of the therapeutic process.

The relational revolution's most profound contribution lies in fostering a new humility among practitioners. By insisting that interpretation emerges from the intersubjective field rather than being imposed from above, relational theorists have encouraged analysts to question the epistemological foundations of their knowledge. This shift represents not merely a technical adjustment but a fundamental reimagining of what it means to understand another person's unconscious life. The recognition that the analyst's personality is not an obstacle to be overcome but an essential instrument to be thoughtfully employed has opened new therapeutic possibilities previously foreclosed by classical strictures.

Perhaps most significantly, the relational approach has expanded the scope of psychoanalytic inquiry to include previously marginalized concerns. Issues of gender, race, social power dynamics, oppression, and discrimination—once considered external to the "real" work of analysis—are now understood as central to psychological development and therapeutic process. This expansion has not only made psychoanalysis more socially conscious but has also deepened our understanding of how cultural and political forces shape individual subjectivity. The consulting room can no longer be imagined as a hermetically sealed space separate from the social world; instead, it becomes a microcosm where larger societal dynamics are both enacted and potentially transformed.

This broadening of perspective has proven particularly vital in attracting a new generation of clinicians who found classical orthodoxy increasingly disconnected from contemporary realities. Young therapists, seeking approaches that acknowledge diversity, question traditional authority, and embrace complexity, have found in relational psychoanalysis a framework that feels both intellectually rigorous and ethically responsive. The movement has succeeded in making psychoanalysis feel relevant and alive rather than preserved in theoretical amber.

The embrace of enactment as inevitable rather than avoidable, the recognition of the analyst's subjectivity as resource rather than contamination—these insights have revolutionized clinical practice. By acknowledging that all meaning is co-created, that interpretation emerges from relationship rather than being imposed upon it, relational theorists have made the therapeutic encounter more genuinely collaborative and potentially transformative.

Yet alongside these considerable achievements, certain tensions have emerged that warrant thoughtful consideration. The very success of the relational approach sometimes leads to what might be called enthusiastic overextension—moments when the valuable emphasis on mutuality risks obscuring the necessary asymmetries that structure therapeutic work. When analysts celebrate "throwing away the book" in moments of crisis, they may sometimes be expressing not clinical flexibility but a concerning abandonment of professional boundaries that some patients desperately need. The patient seeking containment rather than mutuality, interpretive understanding rather than personal revelation, may occasionally find themselves unsettled by an approach that privileges authenticity over structure.

Similarly, there exists a delicate balance between acknowledging the co-created nature of meaning and maintaining the disciplined capacity for psychoanalytic thinking. While the relational critique of false objectivity is invaluable, the complete abandonment of interpretive authority risks losing something essential about the psychoanalytic enterprise—not the problematic certainty of knowing another's unconscious, but the cultivated ability to offer a different perspective, to see patterns the patient cannot yet perceive, and to provide an experience that helps the patient to draw vital distinctions within their inner world and relationships.

The institutionalization of any revolutionary movement presents its own challenges, and the relational school is no exception. As it has evolved from an insurgent critique to an established approach, inevitable tensions have emerged between its egalitarian ideals and the practical necessities of theoretical coherence and clinical training. The movement that arose from resistance to rigid hierarchies must now navigate the complex task of transmitting its insights without creating new orthodoxies, of maintaining theoretical rigor without sacrificing the pluralism it champions.

The path forward likely requires neither uncritical celebration nor wholesale rejection, but rather a mature integration that can hold multiple truths simultaneously. The analyst must be both humble about their limitations and confident in their professional expertise, both aware of their subjective participation and capable of offering something beyond mere mirroring, both socially conscious and psychologically focused. This is not a comfortable position—it requires tolerating paradox and sustaining ambiguity. Yet it is precisely this creative tension that keeps psychoanalysis vital as a living tradition.

The relational revolution has succeeded in making psychoanalysis more democratic without sacrificing depth, more mutual without abandoning professional responsibility, more inclusive without losing specificity. By bringing previously excluded voices and concerns into the psychoanalytic conversation, by questioning the foundations of analytic authority while maintaining respect for clinical wisdom, by embracing complexity while remaining clinically effective, the relational movement has ensured that psychoanalysis remains a relevant and evolving discipline.

The future of psychoanalytic interpretation lies in maintaining this creative tension—between tradition and innovation, authority and mutuality, individual psychology and social consciousness. The relational contribution has provided invaluable tools for navigating these tensions with greater awareness and sophistication. As the movement continues to evolve, its ability to remain self-reflective about its own limitations while building on its considerable strengths will determine whether it continues to inspire new generations of clinicians seeking approaches that are both therapeutically powerful and ethically responsive to our complex world.

References

Aron, L. (1992). Interpretation as expression of the analyst's subjectivity. *Psychoanalytic Dialogues*, 2(4), 475–507.

Bass, A. (2003). "E" enactments in psychoanalysis: Another medium, another message. *Psychoanalytic Dialogues*, 13(5), 657–675.

Benjamin, J. (2004). Beyond doer and done to: An intersubjective view of thirdness. *Psychoanalytic Quarterly*, 73(1), 5–46.

Benjamin, J. (2018). *Beyond doer and done to: Recognition theory, intersubjectivity and the third*. Routledge.

Bollas, C. (1987). *The shadow of the object: Psychoanalysis of the unthought known*. Columbia University Press.

Bromberg, P. M. (2010). Minding the dissociative gap. *Contemporary Psychoanalysis*, 46 (1), 19–31.

Ferro, A., & Civitarese, G. (2015). *The analytic field and its transformations*. Karnac Books.

Greenberg, J. (2001). The analyst's participation: A new look. *Journal of the American Psychoanalytic Association*, 49(2), 359–381.

Kuchuck, S. (2009). Do ask, do tell: Narcissistic need as a determinant of analyst self-disclosure. *Psychoanalytic Review*, 96(6), 1007–1024.

Kuchuck, S. (2018). The Analyst's Subjectivity: On the Impact of Inadvertent, Deliberate, and Silent Disclosure. *Psychoanalytic Perspectives*, 15: 265–274.

Kuchuck, S. (2021). *The relational revolution in psychoanalysis and psychotherapy*. Phoenix Publishing House.

Mills, J. (2017). Challenging relational psychoanalysis: A critique of postmodernism and analyst self-disclosure. *Psychoanalytic Perspectives*, 14(3), 313–335.

Mitchell, S. A. (1988). *Relational concepts in psychoanalysis: An integration*. Harvard University Press.

Mitchell, S. (2000). You've got to suffer if you want to sing the blues: Psychoanalytic reflections on guilt and self-pity. *Psychoanalytic Dialogues*, 10(5), 713–733.

Ogden, T. H. (1994). The analytic third: Working with intersubjective clinical facts. *International Journal of Psycho-Analysis*, 75, 3–19.

Ogden, T. H. (1997). *Reverie and interpretation: Sensing something human*. Jason Aronson.

Ogden, T. H. (2004). The Analytic Third: Implications for Psychoanalytic Theory and Technique. *Psychoanalytic Quarterly* 73, 167–195.

Stern, D. (2009). Shall the twain meet? Metaphor, dissociation, and cooccurrence. *Psychoanalytic Inquiry*, 29(1), 79–90.

Suggested Reading

Aron, L., Grand, S., & Slochower, J. A. (Eds.). (2018). *De-idealizing relational theory: A critique from within*. Routledge.

Chapter 7

Essential Writings on Interpretation

Five Landmarks in the Evolution of Psychoanalytic Thinking

What actually happens in the moment when interpretation transforms suffering into understanding, repetition into recognition, deadness into aliveness? This question—deceptively simple yet endlessly complex—has haunted psychoanalysis since its inception. Each generation of analysts has approached it anew, discovering that what we call "interpretation" is far stranger than our theories suggest.

The five papers (Strachey, Symington, Bollas, Ogden, and Stern) examined in this chapter don't merely answer this question; they progressively complicate it, revealing interpretation to be less a technique we master than an evolving encounter that continually shapes and challenges our understanding.

These contributions span nearly a century, from Strachey's 1934 attempt to isolate the precise mechanism of therapeutic change to Stern's 2023 reconceptualization of interpretation as the voice of an interpersonal field. Together, they trace a remarkable journey: from certainty to uncertainty, from technique to relationship, from knowing to being. Yet this is not a story of progress in any simple sense. Each paper discovers something essential that the others miss, and what emerges is not a synthesis but a productive tension—a recognition that interpretation works in multiple ways simultaneously, often contradicting our conscious intentions.

DOI: 10.4324/9781003590750-8

Part I: The Classical Foundation—Strachey's Mechanical Precision

James Strachey's 1934 paper "The Nature of the Therapeutic Action of Psychoanalysis" stands as one of the most influential works in psychoanalytic literature. What makes this contribution enduring is not merely its systematic approach, but its recognition of a fundamental paradox: therapeutic change requires the analyst to become temporarily part of the patient's internal world while simultaneously remaining sufficiently separate to offer something genuinely new. This delicate balance lies at the heart of what Strachey termed "mutative interpretation."

The originality of Strachey's contribution lies in his distinction between interpretations that merely inform and those that actually transform. Anyone can tell a patient what they are doing unconsciously—this is what he dismissively called "dictionary" interpretation. But mutative interpretation operates through a more complex process involving what Strachey called an "auxiliary superego," a temporarily introjected figure who operates according to different principles than the patient's harsh internal critics (Strachey, 1934, p. 127).

This creates what Strachey identified as a two-phase process of change. During the first phase, the analyst gives permission for small quantities of the patient's forbidden impulses to become conscious, with these impulses directed toward the analyst in the transference. During the second phase, the patient recognizes the difference between their archaic expectations and the analyst's actual response, creating what Strachey called "a breach in the neurotic vicious circle" (Strachey, 1934, p. 159).

True therapeutic change, he argued, occurs through countless small modifications rather than dramatic insights. We can only integrate as much change as our psychic equilibrium can bear. Push too hard, and the patient's defenses mobilize to preserve the status quo. Offer too little, and nothing shifts at all.

The interpretation must achieve optimal dosage—enough to mobilize unconscious material but not so much as to overwhelm the patient's capacity to process the experience. As Strachey emphasizes, the mutative effect depends entirely on this careful calibration of psychological forces.

Strachey's emphasis on transference interpretation as the only truly mutative form has profoundly influenced psychoanalytic technique. Extra-transference interpretations, while useful as "feeders," cannot produce the same structural changes because they lack the immediate emotional charge necessary for genuine transformation. Only in the here-and-now relationship with the analyst can the patient experience the crucial discrepancy between expectation and reality that enables new internal structures to form.

The essential difference lies in the fact that it is only in transference interpretation that the object of the id impulse is present. This makes it difficult for an extra-transference interpretation to be given at the point of urgency, and even if accomplished, it remains problematic whether the patient will be able to establish the difference between the real (absent) object and the fantasy object. An extra-transference interpretation will therefore always be less effective and more risky.

Drawing on Melanie Klein's insights about projection and introjection, Strachey explains both the mechanism of neurosis and its cure. The neurotic becomes trapped in what he calls a "vicious circle" where projected sadism creates increasingly dangerous internal objects, which in turn provoke more defensive sadism. The human being functions through continuous processes of introjection and projection, which lay the foundations both of object relationships and of the structure of the psychic apparatus.

The analyst, however, can function differently. Given the analyst's real behavior and the patient's minimum contact with reality, the patient will incorporate the analyst as an object that differs from the rest—the auxiliary superego. This auxiliary superego differs from the patient's archaic superego in crucial ways. Most importantly, as Strachey notes, "the most important characteristic of the auxiliary super-ego is that its advice to the ego is consistently based upon real and contemporary considerations and this in itself serves to differentiate it from the greater part of the original super-ego" (Strachey, 1934, p. 140).

The fundamental rule itself exemplifies this difference. The auxiliary superego authorizes the patient to say everything that comes into his head—what might be called the abolition of rejection. In this way the new superego ("thou may say") functions in the opposite direction to the old ("thou must not say").

Strachey describes mutative interpretation as consisting of two phases, though these need not occur sequentially and can happen simultaneously. Neither phase is simple and both can be complex, but from a genetic point of view, they will always exist. The key to the theory is that the patient should become conscious of two things: an instinctive impulse and an object that does not tally with that impulse.

During the first phase, a previously unconscious id impulse or its derivative becomes conscious, directed toward the analyst. This may occur directly and spontaneously, but more often the analyst intervenes with a series of interpretations. The ego defense, the superego censure, and the instinctive impulse must be interpreted in various ways until the derivative reaches consciousness and anxiety is mobilized in quantities which must always be moderate.

The second phase depends crucially on the patient's sense of reality, enabling comparison between the real object and the archaic (transferred) one. This comparison is always extremely uncertain—the patient may at any moment turn the real object (analyst) into the archaic one. Here the decisive importance of the analytic setting becomes apparent. If the analyst strays from the setting and behaves inappropriately, the immediate response will be the patient's inclusion of the analyst in the series of good or bad archaic objects, thereby disqualifying the analyst and preventing the second phase.

Strachey outlines three essential characteristics of mutative interpretation. First, it must be immediate—applied to an impulse in a cathected state. An interpretation which informs a patient of the existence of an impulse which is not present can never be mutative, although it may be useful in preparing the ground. A necessary condition will always be that the interpretation relates to an emotion that the patient experiences as actual.

Second, the interpretation must be specific—detailed and concrete rather than vague and general. While broad interpretations may be necessary when tackling new subjects, until we manage to circumscribe the material and put into focus all the relevant details, we can never expect a mutative effect. The interpretation must adapt itself exactly to what is happening; it must be concrete and limited to the point in question.

Third, mutative interpretation must be progressive, proceeding in well-graduated steps. The interpretation must hold to the principle of optimum quantity, because otherwise either the first phase will not be reached or the second will become impossible. Strachey teaches us to distrust hasty interpretations that attempt to skip stages. Upheavals are not mutations, and great changes turn out to be short-lived and suggestive in nature. One of Strachey's most significant contributions lies in his evaluation of extra-transference interpretation. His position is unequivocal: "Is it to be understood that no extra-transference interpretation can set in motion the chain of events which I have suggested as being the essence of psychoanalytical therapy? That is indeed my opinion" (Strachey, 1934, p. 154).

Strachey's framework has continued to exert a remarkable level of influence over decades of psychoanalytic development. Etchegoyen (1983), writing fifty years after the publication of the original paper, notes that "together with many other psychoanalysts, I consider Strachey's contribution to be of very real importance, and that his influence is still extremely strong" (p. 454). The work's enduring significance lies in its integration of theory and technique in what remains a convincing framework for understanding therapeutic change.

However, contemporary analysts have also noted limitations in Strachey's approach (Caper, 1995; Hepburn, 2021). Some argue that his mechanistic language reflects the scientific optimism of his era and may not capture the full complexity of the therapeutic relationship. Others suggest that factors beyond interpretation—including the analyst's personality and the quality of the therapeutic relationship—play more significant roles than Strachey's theory acknowledges.

Despite these critiques, Strachey's fundamental insights remain clinically relevant. His careful distinction between interpretations that inform and those that transform continues to guide analytic practice. His emphasis on the primacy of transference interpretation has shaped generations of analysts' understanding of therapeutic technique. Most importantly, his recognition that structural change occurs through countless small modifications rather than dramatic breakthroughs provides essential guidance for clinical work.

Part II: The Turn to Subjectivity—Inner Freedom as Therapeutic Action

If Strachey provided the mechanics of therapeutic change, Neville Symington revealed something more elusive yet perhaps more fundamental: the analyst's internal freedom as the precondition for any meaningful interpretation. This shift from technique to the analyst's state of mind marked a crucial turn in psychoanalytic thinking, one that would eventually lead to the relational revolution.

Symington's 1983 paper introduces what he calls the "x-phenomenon"—the analyst's internal act of freedom that precedes and enables meaningful interpretation (Symington, 1983, p. 283). This is the freedom to think one's own thoughts while remaining emotionally engaged with the patient. It reflects the capacity to be both inside and outside the patient's projective system simultaneously—a paradox that defines the analyst's impossible but necessary position.

The clinical material Symington presents illuminates this paradox beautifully. In the case of Miss M., a patient for whom he charged significantly less than his usual fee, Symington had unconsciously accepted her self-perception of limitation and inadequacy. For months, he treated this arrangement as an unchangeable fact. The therapeutic breakthrough occurred not through any interpretation but through a spontaneous thought: "Why can't Miss M pay the same as all my other patients?" (Symington, 1983, p. 283). This internal shift preceded any discussion with the patient, yet its effects were immediate and profound. When he eventually raised the fee, Miss M. found better employment and extricated herself from exploitative relationships.

What Symington discovered was that analysts are constantly being "lassoed into" their patients' projective systems (Symington, 1983, p. 283). We become unwitting actors in our patients' internal dramas, playing roles we don't consciously choose. The therapeutic action depends not on avoiding this entanglement—which is impossible—but on achieving moments of freedom from it while maintaining emotional connection. This is a different kind of neutrality than classical analysis imagined: not the neutrality of non-involvement but the neutrality that comes from recognizing one's involvement and achieving momentary freedom from it.

Symington's concept of the "corporate personality"—the fused entity that analyst and patient create at the superego level—anticipates many later relational concepts (Symington, 1983, p. 288). Both participants become trapped in shared illusions comprising the patient's internalized family values and destructive patterns. The analyst's task is not to interpret these patterns from the outside but to achieve freedom from within them, and this internal liberation somehow communicates itself to the patient before any words are spoken.

Part III: Crisis as Communication—The Radical Promise of Breakdown

While Symington focused on freeing the analyst from projective entanglements to think clearly, Christopher Bollas takes this liberation in a radical direction: the analyst's freedom enables complete devotion to creating a holding environment for patients whose psychic organization is collapsing, with this devoted containment itself functioning as interpretation.

Bollas's approach to patients on the verge of breakdown fundamentally challenges conventional psychiatric wisdom. What appears as mental collapse, he suggests, may actually constitute the psyche's most sophisticated attempt at communication—a desperate effort to make known what has never been mentally represented. The breakdown becomes not pathology to be eliminated but text to be interpreted, not a failure to function but the beginning of a profound conversation that has been waiting decades to occur.

Drawing on his deep engagement with Donald Winnicott's ideas about breakdown and breakthrough, Bollas developed in his book *Catch Them Before They Fall: The Psychoanalysis of*

Breakdown (2013) a method that pushes the boundaries of traditional analytic practice. This involves offering patients already in analysis an extraordinary therapeutic contract when breakdown threatens. He proposes meeting twice daily at no extra cost—a radical departure from conventional practice that reflects his understanding that patients on the verge of collapse cannot cope with additional stressors, particularly the anxiety of accumulating debt during their most vulnerable moments (Bollas, 2013). The financial arrangement itself becomes part of the interpretation: it communicates that the analyst recognizes the gravity of the situation and is willing to match the patient's desperation with an equally desperate commitment to understanding.

The contract demands total commitment from both parties. Patients must abandon all other obligations and give absolute priority to the treatment. When patients protest about missing important engagements, Bollas remains firm. The gravity of their condition requires absolute seriousness—a form of sanctuary where psychoanalysis can be intensified and the character of the breakdown allowed full articulation. This stringency is not authoritarian control but recognition that breakdown operates according to its own temporal logic that cannot be subordinated to social conventions.

Bollas's (2013) clinical work demonstrates how interpretation during breakdown must operate simultaneously at multiple levels. In the case of Anna (pp. 46–59), a patient who had maintained a facade of perfection while harboring violent hatred toward her mother, Bollas offers interpretations that address both the content of her psychological crisis and the form of the breakdown itself. He tells her slowly and calmly that her breakdown was inevitable, that it represents the return of dissociated aspects of self that could no longer be kept at bay. This communication proves essential because patients in breakdown must deal not only with the traumatic material that triggered the collapse but also with secondary panic over the fact of breaking down itself.

Building on Winnicott's revolutionary understanding that breakdown can contain the seeds of breakthrough, Bollas develops a more systematic approach to the interpretive challenges posed by patients in extremis. Where Winnicott emphasized the analyst's survival of the patient's destructive attacks, Bollas focuses on the interpretive dimension—reading the breakdown as meaningful text requiring specialized hermeneutic skills. The analyst must interpret not only what the patient says but what the collapse itself communicates about chronically unmet needs.

For Bollas, interpretation becomes a form of love—being known is being loved at a crucial time in one's life. Each interpretive step constitutes part of what he calls "psychoanalytical holding." People feel understood not simply through empathic presence but through the intelligent grasp the analyst has of why this particular person is in their particular predicament. This perspective requires extraordinary faith in the interpretive process itself—a conviction that understanding alone possesses sufficient therapeutic power to prevent psychological collapse.

His opposition to hospitalization and intensive medication reflects his belief that these approaches fundamentally misinterpret the nature of breakdown. By treating collapse as pathology requiring suppression rather than communication requiring understanding, conventional psychiatric responses negate the breakdown's transformative potential. Bollas positions himself as someone who can recognize the signs of impending collapse and intervene interpretively before the breakdown becomes irreversible—catching them, as the title of his 1983 book suggests, before they fall.

This approach raises profound questions about the limits of interpretive responsibility. Some patients, Bollas suggests, require analysts willing to risk everything—their conventional technique, their professional boundaries, their personal comfort—in service of interpretive understanding. His work represents a profound act of faith in the transformative power of being deeply understood, even when understanding must be achieved at the very edge of psychological collapse.

Part IV: From Knowing to Being—The Ontological Turn

The progression from Bollas's intensive engagement with breakdown to Thomas Ogden's ontological psychoanalysis represents another fundamental shift in how we understand interpretation.

Where Bollas demonstrates interpretation under extreme conditions, Ogden questions whether interpretation, as traditionally conceived, might sometimes be precisely what prevents genuine therapeutic change.

Ogden's distinction between epistemological and ontological psychoanalysis captures a transformation in therapeutic sensibility that had been quietly developing over decades (Ogden, 2019, p. 663). Epistemological psychoanalysis, associated primarily with Freud and Klein, focuses on knowing and understanding unconscious meanings. Ontological psychoanalysis, championed by Donald Winnicott and Wilfred Bion, centers on being and becoming—on the struggle to come into existence as a person who feels real and alive to oneself.

If the goal is helping patients to become more fully themselves rather than simply understanding their unconscious conflicts, then the analyst's primary task becomes creating conditions whereby patients can discover meaning creatively and with joy, rather than having meaning delivered to them by someone who knows. Winnicott's confession that his personal need to interpret had prevented or delayed deep change reveals the potential violence of epistemological enthusiasm (Ogden, 2019, p. 664).

Ogden's clinical examples illuminate this distinction with remarkable clarity. When he asked a patient who hadn't spoken to his father for a year, "Haven't you had enough of that by now?" the intervention addressed not the content of the conflict but the patient's state of being (Ogden, 2019, p. 674). The question implied that through analysis the patient had become someone for whom not talking to his father no longer reflected his true self. The patient called his father that evening and later told Ogden that this moment fundamentally altered who he was.

This intervention's power lies in its ontological precision. Ogden wasn't interpreting unconscious meaning but recognizing and reflecting the person the patient had become through their work together. The interpretation emerged from awareness of the patient's essential being rather than from theoretical knowledge about father-son relationships.

Perhaps most moving is Ogden's work with Mr. C., a man with cerebral palsy whose mother had rejected him as a "slobbering monster" (Ogden, 2019, p. 680). Years into treatment, Mr. C. shared a dream of washing his car while enjoying music—a simple scene of himself with cerebral palsy engaged in ordinary activity with pleasure. Rather than analyzing symbolic content, Ogden simply said, "What a wonderful dream that was" (Ogden, 2019, p. 680). This response honored the patient's achievement of self-acceptance, celebrating being rather than seeking understanding.

Bion's contribution to ontological thinking appears in his emphasis on experiencing over understanding. His advice to cultivate "a watchful avoidance of memory" reflects his belief that memory represents what we think we know based on what no longer exists (Ogden, 2019, p. 669). For Bion, analysts don't come to know what's happening in sessions but "intuit" it, becoming "at one" with it.

Bion's conception of reverie—a state of unconscious receptivity to the patient's undreamable experience—exemplifies ontological thinking. The analyst doesn't interpret the patient's projective identifications but becomes temporarily transformed by them, offering back a "dreamt" version of what was previously unthinkable. This represents a fundamentally different way of being with patients' psychotic anxieties.

This ontological turn reflects broader philosophical shifts from Cartesian subject-object dualism toward phenomenological and existential frameworks. The patient is no longer an object to be understood but a fellow being struggling toward authentic existence. Ontological psychoanalysis suggests that our patients come to us not primarily seeking understanding but hoping to become more fully themselves.

Importantly, Ogden emphasizes that epistemological and ontological approaches coexist in "'mutually enriching relationship." The question isn't whether to interpret but how interpretation can serve the patient's becoming rather than the analyst's need to understand. This reframes interpretation not as delivery of insight but as participation in the patient's creative discovery of meaning.

Our interpretations matter not because they reveal hidden truths but because they create new possibilities for being. The deepest answer to Winnicott's question—"What do you want to be when you grow up?"—may simply be: "Myself, but more so."

Part V: The Relational Synthesis—Interpretation as Emergent Property

Donnel Stern's field theory of interpretation represents both a culmination and a new beginning in psychoanalytic thinking about therapeutic action. His observation that former patients almost never report remembering specific interpretations but instead recall moments of feeling deeply understood challenges decades of theoretical emphasis on interpretation as the primary agent of change (Stern, 2023, p. 1127). Yet rather than diminishing interpretation's importance, Stern reconceptualizes it as something more mysterious and more powerful than we had imagined.

Stern's radical proposition is that interpretations are not the analyst's conscious creations, but rather they are "the voice of the field"—expressions of the dynamic interpersonal space between analyst and patient. The field functions like a changing screen that selects which parts of each person's mind can be engaged at any given moment (Stern, 2023, p. 1136).

This reconceptualization builds on Edgar Levenson's foundational insight that "language is no less a form of conduct than a form of meaning"; analysts, he suggests, cannot describe unconscious patterns without simultaneously enacting them (Stern, 2023, p. 1132). Drawing also on Winnicott's focus on being rather than knowing, and Bromberg's theatrical metaphors of shifting self-states, Stern synthesizes decades of relational thinking into a coherent field theory. The approach challenges classical notions of interpretive neutrality, positioning the analyst as embedded participant rather than detached observer.

The therapeutic value of interpretation stems primarily from widening and deepening the patient's sense of being known by someone who has become emotionally significant (Stern, 2023, p. 1128). This process of "witnessing" involves not just recognition but "coming into possession of oneself"—experiencing not only that one's experience is one's own but also knowing and feeling that it is we who are doing the knowing and feeling. This dual awareness constitutes the core of therapeutic action.

Drawing on Edgar Levenson's insight that psychoanalysis is the attempt to grasp what analyst and patient are "up to" in their relationship, Stern recognizes that analysts cannot separate themselves from the patterns they observe (Stern, 2023, p. 1132). Every time they speak, they are interacting from within the same configurations they wish to name. This challenges the traditional view of the analyst as objective observer, positioning them instead as participant-observer caught up in the very dynamics they seek to understand.

Stern's clinical example with Alan illustrates these concepts elegantly. During a phone session, Alan indirectly expresses irritation when Stern abruptly ends their call. Through subtle interaction—Alan's sardonic laugh and Stern's recognition of it—a shift occurs in their field that allows both to acknowledge Alan's feeling. Stern's interpretation addresses not just the irritation but the relational pattern it reveals (Stern, 2023, p. 1141). What makes this transformative is that Alan "saw me seeing him" without responding with shame or retaliation (Stern, 2023, p. 1144).

Following this moment, Alan begins expressing anger toward his narcissistic mother for the first time and makes significant changes in self-care. Stern emphasizes that this movement occurred precisely because neither could say why it happened—the fact that they did something unexpected together is the point (Stern, 2023, p. 1145).

This view places interpretation firmly in the realm of ontology rather than epistemology. As Bromberg notes, interpersonal novelty allows the self to grow because it is unanticipated by both persons, organized by what takes place between two minds, and belongs to neither person alone (Stern, 2023, p. 1145).

Conclusion: The Paradox of Therapeutic Action

These five papers attempt to isolate the mechanism of therapeutic change, revealing new layers of complexity, and new paradoxes that resist resolution. Strachey showed us the precision of mutative interpretation, only for Symington to reveal that the most important therapeutic action might occur before any interpretation is spoken. Bollas demonstrated interpretation at the edge of breakdown, while Ogden suggested that sometimes not interpreting might be the most profound intervention. Stern completed the circle by proposing that interpretation belongs fully to neither analyst nor patient but emerges from the field they create together.

What remains constant across these contributions is the recognition that something happens in psychoanalysis that exceeds our theoretical understanding. Whether we call it the auxiliary superego, the act of freedom, the reading of breakdown, ontological recognition, or the voice of the field, each theorist points toward a process that is simultaneously precise and mysterious, technical and deeply human.

Perhaps this is interpretation's essential paradox: it works best when we understand least why it works. The moment we think we've mastered interpretive technique, we've likely lost touch with what makes interpretation transformative. Our patients don't need our clever insights nearly as much as they need our capacity to be surprised by them, to discover with them something neither of us could have found alone.

The clinical implications are profound. These papers suggest that becoming a skilled interpreter requires not accumulating techniques but developing capacities—the capacity to achieve internal freedom while remaining engaged, to read breakdown as communication, to recognize being as more fundamental than knowing, to hear the voice of the interpersonal field. These are not skills that can be taught directly but sensibilities that develop through the repeated experience of being transformed by our patients even as we participate in transforming them.

The question that opened this exploration—what happens in the moment when interpretation transforms suffering into understanding, repetition into recognition, and deadness into aliveness?—remains beautifully unanswered. Each paper offers a partial view, a fragment of understanding that illuminates one aspect while casting others in shadow. Together, they suggest that interpretation is less something we do than something that happens through us when we create the right conditions. It is both art and science, technique and intuition, precision and mystery.

In the end, these five landmarks in psychoanalytic thinking about interpretation teach us something essential: that our most powerful therapeutic tool may not be our knowledge or our technique but our capacity to remain open to being surprised by the depth and complexity of human experience. The interpretation that transforms is often the one we didn't plan to make, emerging from a moment of genuine meeting between two people willing to risk being changed by their encounter. This is perhaps why former patients remember not our brilliant interpretations but the moments when they felt truly seen—because in those moments, interpretation transcends technique and becomes recognition, witness, and ultimately, love.

References

Bollas, C. (2013). *Catch them before they fall: The psychoanalysis of breakdown*. Routledge.

Caper, R. (1995). On The Difficulty Of Making A Mutative Interpretation. *International Journal of Psychoanalysis*, 76, 91–101.

Etchegoyen, R. H. (1983). Fifty years after the mutative interpretation. *International Journal of Psychoanalysis*, 64, 445–459.

Hepburn, J. M. (2021). Strachey's Shadow: A Re-Examination of the Use of the Mutative Interpretation. *British Journal of Psychotherapy*, 37, 195–207.

Ogden, T. H. (2019). Ontological psychoanalysis or "What do you want to be when you grow up?". *Psychoanalytic Quarterly*, 88, 661–684.

Stern, D. B. (2023). Interpretation: Voice of the field. *Journal of the American Psychoanalytic Association*, 71, 1127–1148.

Strachey, J. (1934). The nature of the therapeutic action of psychoanalysis. *International Journal of Psychoanalysis*, 15, 127–159.

Symington, N. (1983). The analyst's act of freedom as agent of therapeutic change. *International Review of Psychoanalysis*, 10, 283–291.

Afterword

The Interpretive Paradox

After a century of refining psychoanalytic interpretation, we face an uncomfortable irony: the more we understand about therapeutic change, the less certain we become about what makes interpretation work. Each major tradition we've examined has claimed to solve the puzzle, only to reveal new layers of complexity that resist our attempts at mastery.

Freud's archaeological model, with its emphasis on making the unconscious conscious, coexisted uneasily with his growing recognition that insight alone rarely produces lasting change. Melanie Klein's technique of immediate interpretation reflected her belief that primitive anxieties could be directly addressed, yet she simultaneously acknowledged the complex defensive operations that make such communication treacherous. Wilfred Bion's discovery that withholding interpretation could be more transformative than offering it emerged from his deeper understanding of containment and the analyst's function as a thinking apparatus. Heinz Kohut's emphasis on empathic understanding arose from his recognition that interpretation must occur within a context of emotional safety and recognition. Contemporary relationalists' focus on co-created meaning reflects their understanding that all interpretation is inevitably shaped by the subjectivities of both participants.

Bruce Reis (2023), in his masterful survey of contemporary approaches, offers us a provocative distinction: some interpretations aim at content, others at action. Some tell us what things mean; others do something in the telling.

DOI: 10.4324/9781003590750-9

Yet in clinical practice, these distinctions collapse in illuminating ways. The interpretation that appears to reveal hidden content simultaneously transforms the patient's capacity to bear previously unbearable experience. The empathic response that seems purely supportive nevertheless reorganizes internal structures through the very act of being understood. The silence that looks like absence of interpretation becomes the most profound interpretation possible.

Perhaps what we're discovering is that every taxonomy of interpretation reveals more about our need to organize mystery than about the mystery itself. We divide interpretations into categories—epistemological, transformative, developmental, enactive, aesthetic—but in the consulting room they blend and blur like watercolors in the rain.

This convergence points toward something fundamental: interpretation works through relationship rather than accuracy. Whether we call this process insight, containment, empathy, or co-creation, its therapeutic power lies in demonstrating that subjective reality can be approached, engaged, and survived without catastrophic consequences.

But this raises a troubling question: if interpretation works through relationship rather than accuracy, what prevents psychoanalysis from becoming mere emotional healing rather than psychological understanding? The answer may lie in recognizing that the two are inseparable. Genuine understanding changes the person who understands, just as being truly understood transforms the one who is known. The analyst's knowledge becomes therapeutic when knowing becomes a way of being with the patient that demonstrates new possibilities for being with oneself.

This explains why our most powerful interpretations often surprise us. They emerge from moments when technique temporarily dissolves and something more spontaneous takes its place. These moments feel inevitable yet unexpected, seem to emerge from the relationship itself rather than from either participant alone, and create changes that neither person fully understands but both recognize as significant.

The clinical implications are sobering. We cannot teach students to create such moments, only to recognize and avoid interfering with them when they occur. We cannot supervise the development of interpretive wisdom—we can only help clinicians to become more comfortable with the uncertainty that makes wisdom possible. We cannot master interpretation as technique because interpretation, at its most transformative, transcends technique entirely.

This reframes psychoanalytic training around developing capacities rather than accumulating skills. Students need to develop tolerance for ambiguity, comfort with not knowing, and faith in the therapeutic potential of authentic engagement. They need to learn that their own subjectivity is their most essential instrument, requiring careful attention to how their emotional responses, theoretical preferences, and personal history shape what emerges in treatment.

Perhaps most importantly, they need to discover that the analyst's subjectivity is not an obstacle to understanding but its most essential instrument. The question is not whether to be subjective—this is impossible to avoid—but how to use one's subjectivity in service of the patient's growth rather than one's own comfort. At the same time, such openness to uncertainty must be grounded in rigorous familiarity with psychoanalytic theory and clinical literature, so that intuition and subjectivity are continually informed, disciplined, and challenged by a rich internal repertoire of concepts and models.

This brings us to interpretation's final paradox: it becomes most powerful when we hold it most lightly. The analyst who grasps too tightly to interpretive authority may miss the patient's actual communications. The one who becomes too attached to theoretical correctness may sacrifice therapeutic effectiveness. The one who needs too urgently to understand may prevent the patient from discovering their own capacity to make meaning.

After decades of trying to perfect interpretive technique, we've learned that interpretation is ultimately an ethical stance—a commitment to taking seriously another person's subjective experience, even when it confuses or disturbs us. It requires willingness to be changed by our efforts to understand, discovering that knowing another person inevitably transforms our knowledge of ourselves.

The patients who enter our consulting rooms arrive carrying experiences that exceed available language, suffering that resists explanation, and hopes they may not even recognize as hopes. They need us to join them in the difficult work of creating words for the wordless, meaning from the chaotic, and possibilities from the seemingly impossible. Whether we accomplish this through insight, containment, empathy, or relationship matters less than our genuine commitment to the encounter itself.

In this light, interpretation reveals itself as something more modest and more ambitious than our theories suggest. Modest because it claims no special access to truth, no privileged understanding of human nature, no guarantee of therapeutic success. Ambitious because it attempts something remarkable: to prove that human consciousness can meet itself across the gulf that separates one subjectivity from another.

This attempt succeeds when we remain authentically engaged with getting interpretation wrong—when our failures to understand become invitations to understand more deeply, when our limitations become opportunities for genuine encounter, when our theoretical knowledge becomes secondary to our human presence.

That presence, sustained across time and through difficulty, may be what we've been calling interpretation all along.

References

Reis, B. (2023). What is meant by the term interpretation, and what is it for? *Journal of the American Psychoanalytic Association* 71, 1211–1238.

Index

For Product Safety Concerns and Information please contact our EU representative GPSR@taylorandfrancis.com
Taylor & Francis Verlag GmbH, Kaufingerstraße 24, 80331 München, Germany

www.ingramcontent.com/pod-product-compliance
Lightning Source LLC
Chambersburg PA
CBHW070345270326
41926CB00017B/3989